Simo Neri

Alberto Manguel was born in Buenos Aires and has lived in Italy, England, Tahiti, Canada, and currently lives in France. He is the prizewinning author of *Reading Pictures, A History of Reading,* and *The Dictionary of Imaginary Places,* among other works.

Also by Alberto Manguel

Stevenson Under the Palm Trees

With Borges

Reading Pictures

Into the Looking-Glass Wood

A History of Reading

Bride of Frankenstein

News from a Foreign Country Came

The Dictionary of Imaginary Places

A
READING DIARY

Alberto Manguel

PICADOR

FARRAR, STRAUS AND GIROUX

New York

Note: Unless otherwise indicated, all translations are my own. —A.M.

www.picadorusa.com

Picador® is a U.S. registered trademark and is used by Farrar, Straus and Giroux under license from Pan Books Limited.

For information on Picador Reading Group Guides, as well as ordering, please contact Picador.
Phone: 646-307-5626
Fax: 212-253-9627
E-mail: readinggroupguides@picadorusa.com

Excerpts from *Surfacing* appear courtesy of Margaret Atwood.

Library of Congress Cataloging-in-Publication Data
Manguel, Alberto.
A reading diary / Alberto Manguel.
p. cm
ISBN 0-312-42445-0
EAN 978-0-312-42445-9
1. Manguel, Alberto—Diaries. 2. Manguel, Alberto—Books and reading. I. Title.

PN149.9. M36A3 2004
818'.5403—dc22

2004001746

First published in the United States by Farrar, Straus and Giroux

First Picador Edition: December 2005

10 9 8 7 6 5 4 3 2 1

This book is for Craig.

FOREWORD

> . . . that we must laboriously seek the meaning of each word and line, conjecturing a larger sense than common use permits out of what wisdom and valour and generosity we have.
>
> —Thoreau, *Walden*

> Like every person of good taste, Menard abominated such worthless pantomimes, only apt—he would say—to provoke the plebeian pleasure of anachronism or (what is worse) to enthrall us with the rudimentary notion that all ages are the same or that they are different.
>
> —Jorge Luis Borges, *Ficciones*

There are books that we skim over happily, forgetting one page as we turn to the next; others that we read reverently, without daring to agree or disagree; others that offer mere information and preclude our commentary; others still that, because we have loved them so long and so dearly, we can repeat word by word, since we know them, in the truest sense, by heart.

Reading is a conversation. Lunatics engage in imaginary dialogues that they hear echoing somewhere in their minds; readers engage in a similar dialogue provoked silently by the words on a page. Usually the reader's response is not recorded, but often a reader will feel the need to take up a pencil and answer in the margins of a text. This comment, this gloss, this shadow that sometimes accompanies our favorite books, extends and transports the text into another time and another experience; it lends reality to the illusion that a book speaks to us and wills us (its readers) into being.

A couple of years ago, after my fifty-third birthday, I decided to reread a few of my favorite old books, and I was struck, once again, by how their many-layered and complex worlds of the past seemed to reflect the dismal chaos of the world I was living in. A passage in a novel would suddenly illuminate an article in the daily paper; a half-forgotten episode would be recalled by a certain scene; a single word would prompt a long reflection. I decided to keep a record of these moments.

It occurred to me then that, rereading a book a month, I might complete, in a year, something between a personal diary and a commonplace book: a volume of notes, reflections, impressions of travel, sketches of friends, of events public and private, all elicited by my reading. I made a list of what the chosen books would be. It seemed important, for balance, that there be a little of everything. (Since I'm nothing if not an eclectic reader, this wasn't too difficult to accomplish.)

Reading is a comfortable, solitary, slow and sensuous task. Writing used to share some of these qualities. However, in recent times the profession of writer has acquired something of the ancient professions of traveling salesman and repertory actor. Writers are called upon to perform one-night stands in faraway places, extolling the virtues of their own books instead of toilet brushes or encyclopedia sets. Mainly because of these duties, throughout my reading year I found myself traveling to many different cities and yet wishing to be back home, in my house in a small village in France, where I keep my books and do my work.

Scientists have imagined that, before the universe came into being, it existed in a state of potentiality, time and space held in abeyance—"in a fog of possibility," as one commentator put it—until the Big Bang. This latent existence should surprise no reader, for whom every book exists in a dreamlike condition until the hands that open it and the eyes that peruse it stir the words into awareness. The following pages are my attempt to record a few such awakenings.

2002

JUNE

Saturday

We have been in our house in France for just over a year, and already I have to leave, to visit my family in Buenos Aires. I don't want to go. I want to enjoy the village in summer, the garden, the house kept cool by the thick ancient walls. I want to start setting up the books on the shelves we have just had built. I want to sit in my room and work.

On the plane, I pull out a copy of Adolfo Bioy Casares's *The Invention of Morel*, the tale of a man stranded on an island that is apparently inhabited by ghosts, a book I read for the first time thirty, thirty-five years ago.

This is my first visit to Buenos Aires since the December crisis of 2001, which unhitched the peso from the dollar, saw the economy crash and left thousands of people ruined. Downtown, there are no visible signs of the disaster except that, just before nightfall, the streets fill with hordes of *cartoneros*—men, women and children who scrape a living by collecting recyclable rubbish off the sidewalks. Perhaps most crises are invisible: there are no attendant pathetic fallacies to help us see the devastation. Shops close, people look haggard, prices jump, but overall life carries on: the restaurants are full, the shops still stock expensive imports (though I overhear one woman complaining, "I can't find *aceto balsámico* anywhere!"), the city bustles noisily long past midnight. A tourist in a city that was once my own, I don't see the growing slums, the hospitals lacking supplies, the bankruptcies, the middle class joining soup-kitchen queues.

My brother wants to buy me a new recording of Bach's *Magnificat*. He stops at five bank machines before one agrees to release a few bills. I ask, What will he do when he can't find an obliging machine? There will always be at least one, he says, with magical confidence.

The Invention of Morel begins with a phrase now famous in Argentine literature: "Today, on this island, a miracle happened." Miracles in Argentina appear to be quotidian. Bioy Casares's narrator: "Here are neither hallucinations nor images: merely real men, at least as real as myself."

Picasso used to say that everything was a miracle, and that it was a miracle one didn't dissolve in one's bath.

Later

I walk past Bioy Casares's apartment, next to the cemetery of La Recoleta, where the blue-blooded families of Argentina lie buried in ornate mausoleums topped with weeping angels and broken columns. Bioy Casares, whose novels (whether set on faraway islands or in other cities) chronicle the phantasmagoric atmosphere of the city where he always lived, disliked La Recoleta; he found it absurd that anyone should persist in being snobbish after death.

I find Buenos Aires a ghostly place now. Gombrowicz, who came to this city from Poland in the late 1930s and left twenty-four years later, wrote on the ship that was taking him away forever, "Argentina! In my dreams, with half-shut eyes, I search for her once again within myself—with all my strength. Argentina! It is so strange, and all I want to know is this: Why did I never feel such passion for Argentina in Argentina itself? Why does it assault me now, when I am far away?" I understand his perplexity. Like an ancient ruined city, it haunts you from a distance. Here the past is present in layers, generation after generation of ghosts: the people of my childhood, my disappeared schoolmates, the battered survivors.

In the *Magnificat*, the choir overlaps countless repetitions of *"omnes, omnes generationes,"* crowd after crowd of the dead rising to bear witness.

In Buenos Aires itself, people don't see the ghosts. People seem to live here in a state of mad optimism: "It can't get worse"; "Something will come up." Remy de Gourmont (to whom Bioy Casares owed an unacknowledged debt): "We must be happy, even if it is only for the sake of our pride."

Silvia, my old classmate, tells me that in my school is a plaque to the students murdered by the military. She says I'll recognize several names.

Sunday

Argentinians have long bragged about their so-called *viveza criolla*, or endemic cunning. But this trickster mentality is a double-edged weapon. In literature its incarnation is Ulysses, who was for Homer a clever hero—savior of the Greeks, scourge of Troy, victor over Polyphemus and the Sirens—and for Dante a liar and a cheat condemned to the eighth circle of Hell. Though lately Argentinians seem to have confirmed Dante's dictum, I wonder if it's still possible to revert to Homer's vision and use this dangerous gift in order to vanquish prodigies and overcome obstacles. I'm not optimistic.

Last December, in an angry article in *Le Monde*, I ended by saying that now "Argentina is no longer and the bastards who destroyed it are still alive." An indignant Argentinian psychoanalyst compared my conclusion to that of the European and American bankers who rejected all guilt for the downfall of the country and saw in it some kind of just retribution for Argentinian arrogance. Such an inane comparison is perhaps due to the psychoanalyst's own inability (like that of most Argentinians) to accept the fact that, if anything is to change, the country must redefine itself and, above all, establish an unimpeachable justice system.

Evening

The experience of everyday life is negated by what we want it to be, negated in turn by what we hope it really is.

The unnamed narrator of Bioy Casares's novel is on the run after committing an unspecified crime, always believing that even here on this distant island, lost somewhere in the Caribbean, "they" will come and catch him. And at the same time, he more or less expects miraculous events: salvation, food, falling in love. From within the character, flight and fancy are coherent; from without, it is like watching the unfolding of a mad double reality, two-headed and contradictory.

The physical reality of the island confirms the narrator's impressions of nightmare, except that these are filtered, of course, through that same narrator's eyes. I sit in a café. Coffee is served with packets of sugar bearing the faces of famous twentieth-century characters. I can choose between Chaplin and Mandela. Someone has left an empty Che Guevara sugar packet in the ashtray. Afterward, I walk by a fresh pasta shop called La Sonámbula, "The Sleepwalker." The window of a prêt-à-porter is empty except for a large sign: *Todo debe desaparecer*—"Everything must disappear." Outside a pharmacy, a woman with a doctor's prescription in her hand is asking those who enter to buy her the medicine she needs, because she has no money.

Bioy Casares's narrator has been warned not to attempt to reach the island because of a mysterious disease that (rumor has it) infects all those who land there, killing "from outside inwards." The nails and hair fall out, the skin and the corneas die, and the body lives on for some eight to fifteen days. The surface dies before the inner core. The people he sees are, of course, only surface.

But why keep a diary? Why write down all these notes? The mysterious master of the island, Morel, explains his reasons for keeping a record of his memories: "To lend perpetual reality to my sentimental fantasy."

I miss my new garden in France, my new walls.

Monday

Bioy Casares—aristocratic, intellectual, lady-killer Bioy Casares—describes or foresees the world of the common victim: a literary victim, of course, pursued by literary misfortunes. A Cuban friend once told me that, in Cuba, Bioy Casares is read as a political fabulist; his stories are seen as denunciations of those unjustly condemned, hunted down, all those who suffer the fate of exiles and refugees. "I'll show how the world, by perfecting the police, the use of identity papers, the press, wireless, customs, renders any judicial error irreparable, and is now one undivided hell for all those who are persecuted." The tone (the words are spoken by the narrator) was meant to be self-pitying; today they have a documentary ring. I wonder what Bioy Casares would have thought of this reading, he who considered the label *écrivain engagé* a damning insult.

In *The Invention of Morel*, everything is told hesitatingly. The old trick: verisimilitude in fiction is achieved through a pretended lack of certainty.

Midday

I meet Silvia at La Puerto Rico, the café my friends and I used to go to when we were in high school. It hasn't changed: the wood-paneled walls, the round gray stone tables, the hard chairs, the smell of roasted coffee, perhaps even the same waiters, agelessly old, in stained white smocks. Silvia describes the state of the country as an adolescence come once again. More ghosts, studying for exams at that table, waiting for a friend at that other one, making plans for summer camp at the one over there—all people now disappeared, dead, lost.

In Morel's villa, which he calls a museum, the library contains (with one exception) only works of fiction: novels, poetry, drama. Nothing "real."

The English-speaking reader has not yet discovered the works of Bioy Casares. Though his books are published in the United States they are not read, and the first (perhaps only) novel by Bioy Casares published in England was *The Dream of the Heroes*, in 1986. The ignorance of the English-speaking reader never ceases to amaze me.

Tuesday

The magazine stands are full of glossy publications that track the lives of the rich and famous in exultant banality. Life carries on. Alfred Döblin ends his exile journal back in Baden-Baden after the war and remarks of his fellow Germans, "They have not yet experienced what it is they have experienced."

My sister, who is a psychoanalyst and one of the most intelligent people I know, tells me that almost all of her patients are undergoing a crisis. But there is also a resurgence of the creative impulse: dozens of new literary and political magazines have appeared, and theater and film have acquired a new life. The country's downfall has mysteriously given birth to a palpable atmosphere of creativity, as if artists and writers had suddenly decided to conjure up from the dust that which has been stolen from them.

Morel reminds me of certain characters (Gloria Swanson in *Sunset Boulevard* or the faithful daughter in Merchant-Ivory's *Autobiography of a Princess*) who spend their days watching the past come to life on a screen. The theme of the loved one recalled as a projected image appears for the first time, as far as I know, in an 1892 Jules Verne novel, *The Carpathian Castle* (which, according to Gavin Ewart, inspired Bram Stoker's *Dracula*). In Verne's version, the eccentric Baron Gortz brings back to life the beautiful opera singer Stilla, who has died in the middle of her farewell performance, and with whom the Baron has been long and obsessively in love. In the end, it is revealed that what the Baron has re-created is not her flesh and blood, but merely her image captured on a glass pane, and her voice in a recording.

(I now remember an earlier example: the shadows in Plato's cave.)

Bioy Casares follows the precepts of the detective novel: hide nothing from the very beginning, reveal nothing until the last possible moment. (Although, in *The Invention of Morel*, the revelation appears almost exactly halfway through the novel.)

The projected images of characters from Morel's past repeat prerecorded conversations. In one of these (overheard by the narrator), Morel proposes as a subject the theme of immortality. A false clue, since immortality is not merely persistence. I'm reminded of the clinical nomenclature of the inability to forget: "perseverance of memory."

Proust: "Everything must return, as it is written on the dome of Saint Mark's, and as it is proclaimed, while they drink from the marble and jasper urns on the Byzantine pillar capitals, by the birds that signify both death and the Resurrection."

I had a discussion with Stan Persky on immortality. He argues against the alarms of dystopians that scientific advances will lend us, if not eternal life, at least the possibility of a lengthy enjoyment of the present. I'm not sure; I don't know if I want to go on for a very long time, a time beyond eighty or ninety years (already a small eternity). As I begin to glimpse the certainty of an end, I enjoy all the more the things I've grown accustomed to—my favorite books, voices, presences, tastes, surroundings—partly because I know I won't be here forever. Stan says that, given a sound body and mind, he happily wants this life to continue.

In his journals, Bioy Casares recounts the funeral of the novelist María Luisa Levinson. Her body was displayed in a covered coffin with a small window. Someone remarked that there seemed to be sheets of newsprint covering her face. Her daughter explained that they had put pages from several newspapers inside, "so that if, in the future, the coffin was opened, people would know by the obituaries who was there."

Later

I find it difficult to understand how, living in the Buenos Aires of my childhood, I saw nothing of what was to come later. Swedenborg says that the answers to our questions are all laid out for us, but that we don't recognize them as such because we have in mind other answers. We see only what we expect to see. What then was I expecting when I was eight, ten, thirteen?

I remember the long conversations in cafés, in someone's room after school, walking down so many streets. A peculiar humor permeated all that talking: irony tinged with sadness, absurdity with gravitas. The people of Buenos Aires seemed to possess the capability of enjoying the smallest casual offering, and feeling the most subtle moments of misery. They had a passionate sense of curiosity, a keen eye for the revealing notion and respect for the intelligent mind, for the generous act, for the enlightened observation. They knew who they were in the world and felt proud of that imagined identity. Most important, there was in all this the *possibility* of a blossoming, a ripening. Economic constraints and their attendant politics, imposed from abroad by foreign companies not yet multinational, dictated many of the codes of society, and yet the questioning spirit of Argentinians, their particular wit, their melancholic bravery, held for their society something greater and better, beyond what seemed like passing spells of fraudulent governments. If misfortune struck, as it does sometimes anywhere on earth, then (Argentinians believed) it wouldn't last long; our country was too rich, too strong, too full of promise to imagine an endlessly bleak future.

Leopoldo Lugones, writing in 1916: "Politics! That is the national scourge. Everything in this country that stands for regression, poverty, iniquity, either stems from it or is exploited by it."

Today, at breakfast, my brother tells me that "only" 10 percent of the judiciary system is corrupt. "Of course," he adds, "excluding the Supreme Court, where every single member is venal."

Wednesday

Perhaps out of modesty, Bioy Casares, ardently Argentinian, lends his hero a Venezuelan nationality. *The Invention of Morel* ends with a nostalgic recapitulation of what the narrator's homeland means to him. It is an enumeration of places, people, objects, moments, actions, snatches of an anthem . . . I could do the same to remember Buenos Aires.

Things I remember:

- the scarlet of the ten-peso bill
- different kinds of rolls sold at the baker's: *pebete* (sweetish, brioche-like dough), *fugaza* (flat, crusty), *miñón* (smaller and crustier)
- the scent of the eau de cologne the barber patted onto my father's face at the shop in Harrods
- a comic radio show on Sunday midday: *La Revista Dislocada*
- the sepia-colored girlie magazines sold under the arches of Puente Saavedra
- the tiny turkey sandwiches at the Petit Café
- a strong smell of ammonia around the huge rubber trees of Barrancas de Belgrano
- the sound of the soda cart over the cobblestones outside my window
- the soda siphon and the bottle of wine on the dinner table
- the smell of chicken broth before lunch
- the large steamers moored at the port, reeking of smoke, ready to cross the Atlantic
- jacaranda trees in the early spring mornings

One of the earliest poems I learned by heart was Heine's "*Ich hatte einst ein schönes Vaterland*" ("Once I had a lovely homeland").

Thursday

Memory as nightmare: the narrator of *The Invention of Morel* dreams of a brothel of blind women that (he says) he once visited in Calcutta. In the dream, the brothel becomes a rich, stuccoed Florentine palazzo. Here in Buenos Aires, I dream in Spanish of people who never speak and can't hear me, and always of the city I knew, never as it is now. In my dreams, Avenida 9 de Julio ends at Avenida Santa Fe.

Bioy Casares's narrator has the impression that he is merely playing a game, not fighting for his life.

The day after tomorrow, I leave. I have lunch with my nephew Tomás. We talk about the betrayal of Argentina's history, and of his need to keep believing in the possibility of doing something positive. He is thrilled by a line he has read in Simone de Beauvoir: "I discovered with scorn the ephemeral nature of glory."

Perhaps, in order for a book to attract us, it must establish between our experience and that of the fiction—between the two imaginations, ours and that on the page—a link of coincidences.

Monday

I'm back in France. On the plane, I read an article on the so-called Argentine ants. Vicious fighters in their homeland, in Europe these insects have stopped fighting (for some undetermined reason) and with that surplus energy have managed to build a tunnel, six thousand kilometres long, from northern Spain to southern Italy.

Today I start setting up my library.

The shelves are ready, waxed and clean. I realize that before I can put the books in place, I have to open all the boxes, since the subjects are mixed up and I won't otherwise know how much space I need for, say, detective novels or the works of Bioy Casares. In one of the first boxes I find a copy of Bioy Casares's *La otra aventura*, a collection of essays I edited when I worked for the publisher Galerna in Buenos Aires. I was twenty years old, and we were three in the company: the editor, his wife and I. The book is small, 8½ by 17½ centimeters, with a black line drawing on a red background. I remember going to Bioy Casares's house to pick up the manuscript, a bundle of carbon copies, and reading them on the bus back home.

That was in the early months of 1968. Just over thirty years later I saw Bioy Casares again, weeks before his death. He had shriveled into a frail, bony man who mumbled his words, but his eyes were still extraordinarily bright. He told me that he had thought of the plot for a new novel, a fantastic novel. "There will be an island in it," he said. And then, with a smile, "Again."

I have a photo of Bioy Casares aged seventeen, in profile, bearded, classically handsome. I also have one of him at that last meeting, shoulders hunched, cheeks caved in. It isn't certain that Morel would have chosen to preserve the young man rather than the dying one, the image of what was, over the image of what would be. Morel says to the image of his beloved Faustine (with whom the narrator also has fallen in love), "The influence of the future on the past." Exactly.

What others see as our finest achievements are often not what we ourselves see. Edith Sorel once interviewed Marc Chagall in his house in St.-Paul-de-Vence. The painter was in his mid-eighties and was living with his second wife, Vava, whom he had married a decade earlier. Edith was asking Chagall about how it felt to be one of the world's most famous artists, when Vava excused herself and left the room for a minute. Chagall quickly grabbed Edith's hand, pointed to his departing wife and, his face glowing with pleasure, whispered, "She's a Brodsky!" For the poor Jewish boy who had grown up in the shtetl of Vitebsk, more than any artistic fame, what filled him with pride was having married the daughter of a rich merchant family.

Who is Faustine? Who was she in Bioy Casares's mind? I've just read that the Argentinian Inés Schmidt became the model for Rosa Fröhlich, the Marlene Dietrich character in *The Blue Angel*, after Heinrich Mann met her in Florence in 1905.

Tuesday

I'm in my library, surrounded by empty shelves and growing columns of books. It occurs to me that I can trace all my memories through these piling-up volumes. Then suddenly everything seems redundant, all this accumulation of printed paper. Unless it is my own experience that isn't necessary. It is like the double reality that the narrator experiences when he quotes Cicero: "The two suns that, as I heard from my father, were seen during the Consulate of Tuditanus and Aquilius." Impossibly, the narrator finds in the house an identical copy of the pamphlet he is carrying in his pocket: not two copies of the same pamphlet but twice the same copy. Double reality obliterates itself; that is why meeting our doppelgänger means that we must die.

Title for an essay: "The Library as Doppelgänger."

The room in which my library is to be lodged seems to me huge, and as the books begin to fill it, even more so. I pick up a collection by the Iraqi poet Bakr Al-Sayyab and read:

> My new room
> Is vast, vaster indeed
> Than my tomb shall be.

For years, for lack of space, I kept most of my books in storage. I used to think I could hear them call out to me at night. Now I stand for a long time among them all, flooded with images, bits of remembered text, quotations in random order, titles and names. I find my early copy of *The Invention of Morel*: the second edition, published by *Sur* in 1948, the year I was born.

Friday

Several days of unpacking, and many weeks more to come. Memories and false memories. I think I remember something in a certain way, distinctly. A note on the endpaper pages of a book I open by chance tells me I'm wrong; the event happened somewhere else, with someone else, at a different time. Bioy Casares's narrator: "Our habits suppose a certain way in which things take place, a vague coherence of the world. Now reality appears to me changed, unreal."

Papers that have fluttered out of my books as I dust: a Buenos Aires tramway ticket (trams stopped running in the late sixties); a phone number and a name I can't place; a line, *"laudant illa sed ista legunt"*; a bookmark from the now defunct Librairie Maspéro in

Paris; a ticket stub for *Grease*; a stub for an Athens–Toronto flight; a bill for books from Thorpe's in Guildford, still in shillings and pence; a sticker from Mitchell's Bookstore in Buenos Aires; a drawing of two ducks or two doves done in red crayon; a Spanish playing card, the ten of clubs; the address of Estela Ocampo in Barcelona; a receipt from a store in Milan for a hat I don't remember ever owning; a passport photo of Severo Sarduy; a brochure from the Huntington Library in Pasadena; an envelope addressed to me on George Street in Toronto.

We don't choose what remains. In the past moments captured by Morel in his ghostly projections persist two abominable pieces of music: "Valencia" and "Tea for Two." My mother had an LP by Sara Montiel singing "Valencia."

Saturday

The fantastic must survive a series of logical or absurd explanations. (Sherlock Holmes: "When you have eliminated the impossible, whatever remains, however improbable, must be the truth.") Bioy Casares's narrator proposes five hypotheses for the strange things he sees: that he is sick with the plague; that he has become invisible through bad air and lack of food; that the people he sees are creatures from another planet, incapable of hearing; that he has gone mad; that the phantoms are his dead friends and the island is a form of purgatory or Heaven. The true solution is presumed to be "scientific."

Bioy Casares (Bioy Casares's own sarcastic voice) intrudes into the narrative: "The possibility of several heavens has been stated; if there were only one and all were forced to go there and a charming couple awaited us with all their literary Wednesdays, many of us would have stopped dying long ago." Also this: "Man and mating can't bear long and intense moments." (Borges must have been thinking of this line when he attributed to Bioy Casares the famous quotation in "Tlön, Uqbar": "Mirrors and mating are abominable, because they multiply the number of men." The two friends, Borges and Bioy Casares, mirrored features of each other in their writings. Both *The Invention of Morel* and "Tlön, Uqbar" were written in the same year, 1940.)

Sunday

Unlike Huxley's "feelies" (films that you can touch or "finger") in *Brave New World*, Morel's projected images can be perceived through the sense of smell as well as by touch (a procedure he says was easily achieved), and through the perception of heat. "No witness will admit that these are images," he boasts to the narrator. He is also certain that his "imitations of people" lack consciousness—"like the characters in a film," he adds. (Like books, I think. Like friends remembered.)

The friends I remember are caught in time, as if captured on film. They (many of them are now dead, disappeared) are still the age at which I last saw them; I doubt if they would recognize me now. They are what I know of the past.

"Who would not distrust someone who said, 'I and my friends are apparitions, a new type of photography'?" As I walked around the Buenos Aires I thought I remembered, the ghosts seemed to ask that same ironic question. In my adolescence, I never had the sense of being in a "remembered" place.

Monday

Foreseeably, reality co-opts fiction. On Morel's island, the walls of the villa are film projections that coincide with the walls built of brick and plaster and cover up any cracks or holes in the real thing. In Bioy Casares's later novel *Plan of Escape*, which takes place on another of his fantasy islands, he imagines a prison in which painted walls create for the inmates the illusion of freedom. History bettered both notions. José Milicúa, a Spanish art historian, has revealed that, during the Spanish Civil War, the Republicans (!) built cells with disturbing murals in the style of Modernist and Surrealist paintings: six feet high, three feet wide and six feet long, hot and airless, and with the cots so angled that the prisoner would fall onto the floor whenever he tried to lie down. An endless loop of the eye-slicing scene in Buñuel's *Un Chien andalou* was projected onto one of the walls. The architect of this nightmare was an Austrian-born Frenchman, Alfonso Laurencic, who called his creations "psychotechnic torture."

Late afternoon

I will sleep one night in the library to make the space truly mine. C. says that this is equivalent to a dog peeing in the corners.

Morel's first idea is to construct an anthology of images exhibited as mementos; that is why the villa is called a museum. He suggests that our technology is constantly inventing machines "to counterbalance absence." Absence, he argues, is merely spatial, and he imagines that every voice, every image produced by those no longer alive is preserved somewhere, forever. One day, he hopes, there will be a machine capable of rebuilding everything, like an alphabet that allows us to understand and compose any possible word. Then, he says, "life will be a storage-room for death." One single advantage for Morel's people-images: they have no memory of the repetition; they relive the moment as if it were always the first time.

It is said that those who don't visit the Chapel of San Andrés de Teixido in Galicia during their lifetime must do so after death. *"A San Andrés de Teixido vai de morto quen non foi de vivo."*

A definition of Hell: Every one of our acts, our utterances, our thoughts preserved since the beginning of time, increasing infinity by an infinite number of infinities, a repetition from which there is no escape.

Thursday

I see (I hadn't remembered) that the narrator hears Faustine speak of Canada, my Canada. Since I became a Canadian citizen in 1985, I've enjoyed finding references to Canada in unexpected places and I've become attentive to capital *C*s on the page. I'm aware that, for Bioy Casares, Canada was equivalent to Shangri-La without the exoticism: mere distance, the archetypal faraway place. It is curious how readers form their own text by remarking on certain words, certain names that have a private meaning, that echo for them alone and are unnoticed by any other. This reminds me of the anonymous reviewer of *Lady Chatterley's Lover* who, in the English magazine *Horse & Hound*, remarked that Lawrence's book contained fine descriptions of the British countryside, unfortunately marred by certain sentimental or erotic digressions.

Hubert Nyssen asks me if I've ever thought that the brain is like a folded codex of almost limitless memory: the mind as book.

Friday

I've finished *The Invention of Morel*, again. Bioy Casares's voice echoes in the room. I pick up his diary to read this evening, before I fall asleep.

The books I take up to my bed at night and the books I sort out in the library during the day are different books. The former impose on me their time and length, their own rhythm of telling before I fall asleep; the latter are ruled by my own notions of order and categories, and obey me almost blindly (sometimes they rebel and I have to change their place on the shelf).

What company will Bioy Casares's novels keep when the library is all set up? In what grouping will I find them? Where will *The Invention of Morel* sit after all these towering columns of books are up on the shelves? (If I keep them in alphabetical order, grouped by language, Bioy Casares's novels will be preceded by the poems of Jaime Gil de Biedma and will be followed by the superb short stories of Isidoro Blaisten.)

I find this comment in Bioy Casares's diary: "I've always said that I write for the reader, but the fact that I continue writing today, when readers (whole-hearted, full-blooded readers) have vanished, proves irrefutably that I write simply for myself."

JULY

Tuesday

I'm on the Eurostar to London. The air conditioning doesn't seem to be working and it's humid and hot. Two women in front of me have been talking ever since we left Paris, too low for me to catch every word but not low enough for me to be able to shut them out. Their voices grate, one especially, and my head is drumming. Then the one with the less grating voice says, quite distinctly, "He curled up in a little ball and died."

A dog? A cat? Was she describing the death of someone she knew? I have the feeling of having walked into a story whose beginning and end I'll never know.

I try to go back to my book, H. G. Wells's *The Island of Dr. Moreau*, in a pocket hardcover Everyman edition I've had since high school. The first time I read *Dr. Moreau* was during the summer holidays. I was twelve, the book a birthday present from my best friend, Lenny Fagin. That was a lucky summer: in the quiet country house we had rented near Buenos Aires, I discovered Nicholas Blake's *The Beast Must Die*, the stories of Horacio

Quiroga, Ray Bradbury's *The Martian Chronicles*. Now Wells was to be added to my desert island hoard.

I knew nothing of either the book or the author; I shared with the protagonist—"Edward Prendick, a private gentleman"—the uncertainty as to what would happen next. I loved the device (which I didn't know was a device) of reading what was meant to be Prendick's own narrative, "found among his papers" after his death. It was like overhearing a private confession, except that I knew I would be told both the beginning (one beginning) and some kind of end. When we are young, stories never seem to conclude on the book's last page.

I don't like people summing up books for me. Tempt me with a title, a scene, a quotation, yes, but not with the whole story. Fellow enthusiasts, jacket blurbs, teachers and histories of literature destroy much of our reading pleasure by ratting on the plot. And

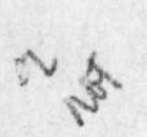

as one grows older, memory, too, can spoil much of the pleasure of being ignorant of what will happen next. I can barely recall what it was like not to know that Dr. Jekyll and Mr. Hyde were one and the same person, or that Crusoe would meet his man Friday.

Lector virgo. That summer, for a few blissful days, I was like Prendick. I knew nothing of the island's history, I dreaded the strange Dr. Moreau, I wrongly suspected the beastly inhabitants of having once been normal human beings, I failed to guess what hideous experiments were going on in the House of Pain. When revelation came, halfway through the book, it proved to be much more dreadful than what I had imagined, and I read on, scared and grateful, to the apocalyptic end.

Such innocent reading, even of books I open for the first time, may no longer be possible.

Wednesday

I'm supposed to be giving a talk tonight, and my publisher has set me up in a small hotel near Soho Square, where Hazlitt once lived. The manager is not terribly friendly; I don't think Hazlitt, not the most patient of men, would have put up with her.

On the second page of *Dr. Moreau* there is a mention of a schooner that sets off from Africa with a puma aboard, and I suddenly remember my first Karl May novel, *The Treasure of the Silver Lake*, which I read when I was six, entranced by the opening scene, in which a panther escapes from its cage aboard a ship crossing a North American lake. In my mind, both scenes are identical.

Note: Reading sometimes consists of making connections, putting together anthologies.

The Soho street outside my window is unbelievably noisy, probably as loud as when Hazlitt lived here. The loudness has an animal quality to it, an idea prompted no doubt by Wells's novel. If I didn't know I was in a city, I might put snouts or beaks to the different screechings, honkings, rumblings, growlings, cacklings, and snarlings I hear. The noise is compounded by the smelly heat that rises from the pavement. London is not at its most pleasant in July. I like Swift's curse concerning London, in his *Stella* journal: "May my enemies live here in summer!"

Late night

Though the setting of *Dr. Moreau* is, of course, the terrible island, in the background is always the idea of its supposed contrast, the civilized city in which Prendick attempts to hide just before the end. I say "supposed" because, for Prendick, London becomes another version of the island nightmare. In his first conversations with Moreau's assistant, Montgomery, Prendick imagines him as "a man who had loved life there, and had been suddenly and irrevocably cut off from it."

I walk through London in the early morning. The patchwork architecture of Soho has an appealing earthiness, a sense of creation by need rather than by committee, a natural hodgepodge quality. Also an obvious hierarchy (rich-poor, expensive-cheap) that the shop signs attempt to conceal.

Aristotle, in the second book of the *Politics*, discussing the six types of political systems that he had imagined for six different kinds of citizens, noted that these systems required a concrete setting of symbolic value in which to develop. The first man to realize this, said Aristotle, was the architect Hippodamus of Miletus, a contemporary of Pericles who, even though he knew nothing of politics, was able to draw up the map of an ideal, well-governed city. Hippodamus's city—or Aristotle's city, since a distance of twenty centuries allows us to confuse an author with his sources—was apparently a reflection of the Greek demographic ideal: a limited number of citizens divided by the roles they play within society.

A list of the characteristics of Aristotle's ideal city would include the following:

- patriarchal, since women have no ruling powers
- democratic, in the sense that affairs of the state are publicly debated, but only by citizens
- military but not expansionist, since the ideal state is by definition a limited space
- elitist, designed for the happiness not of all humanity but of the select citizens whom the Fates have caused to be born on this particular soil, who are therefore justified in using slaves to work under them

Behind the Western notion of a perfect city is the idea of privilege. Moreau, no doubt, would approve.

Thursday

I'm still wondering about the "meaning" of a city like London. Wells didn't like it. In an essay on the future of America, he described London as "a bowl of viscid human fluid [that] boils sullenly over the rim of its encircling hills and slops messily and uglily into the home counties."

With its broken-down transit system and its outrageously high prices, London must be one of the world's most uncomfortable cities for someone with little money to live in. By what advertising means has the British Tourist Board convinced the world that this is not so?

Friday

Dr. Moreau believes that man's will rules life; for Montgomery it's chance. Prendick apparently believes in fate, which is not the same thing. He also believes (or discovers) that fate blurs the line between man and beast. (The famous ending of *Animal Farm*: "The creatures outside looked from pig to man, and from man to pig, and from pig to man again; but already it was impossible to say which was which.")

A pedantic note: the reality of the novel is Kantian. The protagonist sees the world as he imagines it to be, while the reader knows there is a world-in-itself, unknowable to the protagonist. The drama arises from the tension between what the protagonist believes and what the reader knows.

Saturday

Prendick's first walk in the forest (coming upon the strange "savages," then pursued by "the Thing") has an ancient, true ring to it. The forest becomes the tangled place of fairy tales, Dante's dark jungle in which he meets the three wild beasts, the woods through which Orestes is pursued by the Furies.

The book is full of perfect nightmares: "Then something cold touched my hand. I started violently and saw close to me a dim pinkish thing, looking more like a flayed child than anything else in the world."

And of course the haunting ending, in which Prendick describes his attempt to live again in the city after his escape from the terrible island: "I could not get away from men; their voices came through windows; locked doors were flimsy safeguards. I would go out into the streets to fight my delusion, and prowling women would mew after me, furtive craving men glance jealously at me, weary pale workers go coughing by me, with tired eyes and eager paces like wounded deer dripping blood . . ."

Afternoon

In Covent Garden. Out of curiosity, I ask at a bookstore for *The Island of Dr. Moreau*. The clerk wants to know who the author is. I tell him. "Is it recent?" he asks. I explain that it isn't. "If it's more than a month old," he says, "we probably don't have it. But we can maybe order it for you." He looks the title up on the computer. "I can't find it," he says. "It's probably out of print." *Sic transit*.

Sunday

By the time Wells wrote his "scientific romances" (*The Invisible Man*, *The Time Machine*, *The First Men in the Moon*, *The Island of Dr. Moreau*), the utopian ideal had long faded into its shadow image: the dystopia, the place that allows our worst qualities to bloom unhampered, like carnivorous plants.

I remember that as a child I had a vaguely medieval sense of the universe; science and magic presented hazy borders, and the marvels advertised daily in the papers of my childhood (Dr. Salk's polio vaccine, the first television sets in Buenos Aires, the primitive computers, space travel) shared an imaginary bookshelf with Enid Blyton's Wishing Chair and Pinocchio's Land of Laughs. Later, in my adolescence, I trusted those early television series (*The Twilight Zone*, *Boris Karloff Presents*) that depicted the world of science as a dangerous realm of the mind in which unspeakable deeds went unpunished and the stuff of nightmares roamed undisturbed. To me, those series darkly reflected the secret world of adolescence.

Henry James, Sr., in a letter to his sons William and Henry: "Every man who has reached even his intellectual teens begins to suspect that life is no farce; that it is not genteel comedy even; that it flowers and fructifies on the contrary out of the profoundest tragic depths of the essential dearth in which its subject's roots are plunged. The natural inheritance of everyone who is capable of spiritual life is an unsubdued forest where the wolf howls and the obscene bird of night chatters."

Midnight

Just watched *The Bride of Frankenstein* on late-night television, to the sound of police sirens outside my window.

List of mad scientists:

- Dr. Frankenstein
- Rabbi Loew of Prague
- Dr. Moreau
- Dr. Caligari
- Dr. Jekyll
- Captain Nemo
- the Wizard of Oz

Do mad women scientists appear only in fairy tales and myths? Circe? Medea? Snow White's evil stepmother? Hansel and Gretel's witch? Cinderella's fairy godmother?

As these doctors find out, the mad experiments are never final; the thing created always seems to want to return to its original state. Moreau: "Somehow the things drift back again, the stubborn beast flesh grows, day by day, back again . . ."

Note: Keep the allegorical reading out of Wells—Moreau as God, the beast-folk as men. Such a translation seems suspiciously easy. Stay with the pure horror of the adventure.

Here and there, Wells indulges in rhetorical commonplaces: "What could it mean? A locked enclosure on a lonely island, a notorious vivisector, and these crippled and distorted men?" But also beautifully prepared revelations, such as the careful laying out of the beast theme: the dreadful proposal, on the dinghy, to draw lots to see who will be eaten; the medicine that "tasted like blood" and made Prendick feel stronger; the filthy deck strewn with "scraps of carrot, shreds of green stuff," like a cage . . .

Wells is a brilliant name-giver: "The House of Pain." The first time Prendick hears an animal in agony, he finds the cries "irritating," what he calls "the exquisite expression of suffering." One of the Argentinian torturers during the military dictatorship (a cultured man) later declared that he grew accustomed to the "expression of suffering" quite quickly. The sound of the victim, he said, became detached from the person itself, became, as it were, incorporeal, so that it fired in the torturer no feeling of pity or regret, or even the impulse to stop the pain. It was, he said, just "hanging somewhere about."

Dickens, in *Hard Times*: "'Are you in pain, dear mother?' 'I think there's a pain somewhere in the room,' said Mrs. Gradgrind, 'but I couldn't positively say that I have got it.'"

Monday

Crossed back to Paris today. As I disembark at the Gare du Nord, I remember Chesterton's observation: "London is far more difficult to see properly than any other place. London is a riddle. Paris is an explanation."

In the first volume of his *Experiment in Autobiography*, Wells recalls how, at the age of seven, in an old issue of *Chambers' Journal*, he read of a man broken on a wheel. That night he had a horrible dream in which God Himself was turning the instrument of torture. God, the boy concluded, being responsible for everything in the world, must also be responsible for all its evil. Next morning Wells decided that he could no longer believe in the Almighty. The nightmare probably gave him the character of Moreau; in turn, Moreau gave me a healthy fear of doctors and a general distrust of figures of authority.

Borges, when asked if he believed in God: "If the word *God* means a being that exists outside time, I'm not sure I believe in Him. But if it means something in us that is on the side of justice, then yes, I do believe that, in spite of all the crimes, there is a moral purpose to the world."

Tuesday

I remember seeing a photograph of a human ear grafted onto a rat's back, an image that seemed out of Bosch. Dr. Moreau says, "To this day I have never troubled about the ethics of the matter." But the matter *is* ethical, ultimately reflecting our refusal to accept the brutality of death as the concluding chapter.

Vachel Lindsay's "The Leaden-Eyed":

> Let not young souls be smothered out before
> They do quaint deeds and fully flaunt their pride.
> It is the world's one crime its babes grow dull,
> Its poor are ox-like, limp and leaden eyed.
>
> Not that they starve, but starve so dreamlessly,
> Not that they sow, but that they seldom reap.
> Not that they serve, but have no gods to serve,
> Not that they die, but that they die like sheep.

The "gods to serve" troubles me. But those oxlike poor and those who die like sheep are creatures in Moreau's nightmare. "And even it seemed that I, too, was not a reasonable creature, but only an animal tormented with some strange disorder in its brain, that sent it to wander alone, like a sheep stricken with the gid."

Wednesday

Reluctantly finished *The Island of Dr. Moreau*. Though it has lost nothing of its wonderful horror, as I grow older it seems to have become a far more difficult and complex book, crowded with literary allusions. The mad scientist as a Blakean Nobodaddy; the beastly creatures echoing, in reverse, the existential plight of Kafka's metamorphosed Gregor; the island, once as far away as Prospero's, now mapped by postcolonial explorers who see Moreau as the archimperialist—all these are now part of my reading of the story, which the story dutifully accepts and almost immediately outgrows.

Wells attempted, in later life, to give a less fanciful, more serious shape to his ideas. For me, however, his attempt didn't pay off; it's the young scribbler I remember, the author of the "scientific romances" of whom Jules Verne said indignantly, "But this man makes things up!" I remember, together with the awful god Moreau, the Time Traveller who brings from the future an impossible flower, the poor Invisible Man whose eyelids won't shut off the light and whose naked skin won't protect him from the cold, the traitor on the coveted moon. I remember all these necessary inventions that Wells wrote before he was thirty-five. In the next half-century or so he discussed common sense and history, social reform and the theories of education, in earnest books such as *A Modern Utopia*, *The New Machiavelli*, *The Outline of History*, *The Science of Life*. He was still brave and intelligent in difficult times, and honest and sometimes mistaken, and yet by then the gift for myth-making had left him almost completely. One or two stories still made their way to the surface—*The Country of the Blind*, *The Croquet Player*—but by and large the dream source had apparently dried up. It is almost as if the older man, no longer able to imagine, had set out to make books from solid facts, in an effort to recapture what the younger man, inexperienced and untrained, had effortlessly conjured up in intuitions and adventurous visions.

Much as this older reader now tries to recall, though he knows it's impossible, something of the rookie thrill of first reading *The Island of Dr. Moreau*.

AUGUST

Tuesday

My *Kim* belongs to a twenty-five-volume collection, the 1914 Bombay Edition of the works of Kipling (five more volumes were published later) that C. found for me in a secondhand Paris bookstore several years ago. It was the time of the general strike in Paris, which lasted several weeks, and if we needed to do anything downtown we had to walk from the twentieth arrondissement to the center, down streets deserted by buses, past the closed Métro stations, among throngs of curiously amiable and talkative pedestrians. C. had saved up just enough to pay for the collection but hadn't left himself anything for a taxi home. He realized he'd have to traipse several kilometers with the twenty-five volumes on his back, so he reluctantly asked the bookseller whether he could have fifty francs back for the fare. The grumpy old man (may he be denied the coin to pay Charon!) refused, and offered C. instead a large postal bag. With the weight of twenty-five books on his shoulder, C. set off across Paris. He hadn't walked long when a car pulled up and a woman asked him in which direction he was headed. As it happened, she herself was going only a short distance, but when she heard C.'s story she insisted on driving him all the way home.

In the Universal Library, the woman's generosity balances out the bookseller's meanness.

The paper of my *Kim* is a light cream colour, the letters deep black and slightly raised, the initials Prussian blue. Inside each volume is an extra label with the title and volume number, to be used when the book is properly bound (the edition was produced in board bindings, so that each reader might bind it to suit his taste). Rudyard Kipling's signature, on the title page of the first volume, is minuscule, reluctant, perfectly legible.

Kim is one of the few books that constantly delight me; it grows friendlier with each reading. I want to apply to it a word used in Quebec to denote a particular state of happiness: *heureuseté*. I love the tone of the telling, the vividness of every minor character, the moving friendship between the Lama in search of a river and the boy in search of himself. I never want their pilgrimage to end.

Wednesday

The yellow stones of my house reflect the August sun. In the garden, the aspen trees are in bloom, incredibly white. According to De Quincey, "the aspen-tree shivers in sympathy with the horror of the mother tree in Palestine that was compelled to furnish materials for the cross."

The heat of the day here in my village suits the weather in the novel. I watch a pair of turtle doves swoop down onto the grass outside my window, strut around for a moment and then fly back up onto the roof of the pigeon tower at the end of my library. They do this (apparently) for the fun of repetition. Partly, that is why I enjoy rereading.

In *Kim*, everything is given from the very beginning: the inquisitive nature of Kim, the mystery of his past and future, the Lama's quest, the fairy-tale atmosphere evoked by the mention of Harun-al-Rachid and the *Arabian Nights*. There is no confusion or reluctance in the telling of the adventures, except when it becomes deliberately hesitant, to encourage the reader to complete on his own a scene or a dialogue. Otherwise, Kipling knows his story and trusts even its obviousness.

Some time ago, I asked Rohinton Mistry, who, like Kipling, was born in Bombay, to read *Kim*. He had not read it before and was delighted. Like Kipling, Rohinton sees no need, in his own novels, to explain the use of certain words in the Indian vernacular; their meaning shines through in the context and makes the characters' language come alive.

I hate glossaries.

Rohinton told me that he finds Kipling's dialogue, and the descriptions of the vast troupe of Indian characters, absolutely true to life. We wondered whether Kipling made up the proverbs and insults and catchphrases he used in the novel. "Those who beg in silence starve in silence." "Thou hast as much grace as the holy bull of Shiv." "The jackal that lives in the wilds of Mazanderan can only be caught by the hounds of Mazanderan." And so on . . .

Among all the host of minor characters, none is as memorable as the old Indian lady whom Kim and his Lama meet on the Great Trunk Road, who loves good food and gossip, and the thrill of new faces, and who chuckles "like a contented parrot above the sugar lump." She feels *necessary* in the story, as do almost all of the native characters. However, I believe that there is something artificial about the behaviour of the European characters, something impersonal, aloof. But perhaps Kipling was catching a certain false note in the Anglo-Indian mentality. The military historian John Morris noted, "The psychology of the Raj was really based on a lie. The majority of the British in India were acting a part. They weren't really the people they were supposed to be."

When Kipling was a small boy in Bombay, he would be sent by his ayah into the dining room after he was dressed, with the caution "Speak English now to Papa and Mamma." I remember my governess (with whom I spoke English and German) sending me in with a similar recommendation to "speak Spanish" to my parents—a language of which I had only a few halting words.

Thursday

There is a huge, marvelous complexity in Kipling's India that, according to Rohinton, reflects the real thing (I've never been there). Somewhere Kipling says that there are places in the world where, if we wait long enough, everyone will eventually pass. One is King's

Cross Station in London; the other the train station in Bombay. The Great Trunk Road in the novel feels just like such a place. Eliot's "I had not thought death had undone so many" echoes for me the Lama saying, "This is a great and terrible world. I never knew there were so many men alive in it."

Kipling loves lists: carefully chosen names of people, food, objects, gems, clothing are listed, page after page, with a poet's relish. Coleridge: "Poetry = the *best* words in the best order."

That is how Kipling describes the Wonder House: through slow, detailed lists of the sculptures and friezes at the Lahore Museum, stone after stone and image after image, given through the eyes of the Lama, who goes through the collection "with the reverence of a devotee and the appreciative instinct of a craftsman." This is a good description of Kipling's own literary virtues.

This morning we took our friend Katherine Ashenburg (who is visiting us and researching a piece on Romanesque architecture) to see the sculpted white stone portal of the Church of Notre-Dame-la-Grande in Poitiers. Many of the images I found puzzling. Who is the man holding two branches of a tree trunk sprouting from his head? (I found out afterward that this is the Tree of Jesse.) Who is the monster holding his splayed legs, a serpent's head on each foot? Who are the couple embracing or wrestling? Who is the woman carrying an open book? In the small crowd of tourists, I wonder how many of us today see these things with both (or even one) of the Lama's qualities. To be able, like the Lama, to read "incident by incident in the beautiful story . . . on the blurred stone." We have lost most of our vocabularies.

Friday

I've given Katherine an ex-voto embroidered with the hair of a nun (according to the *brocanteur*) to add to the collection of kitschy religious bric-à-brac that she keeps in her bathroom in Toronto. Curiously, for a Catholic, she is able to dissociate herself completely from the supposedly numinous quality of religious objects. Perhaps the contrary impulse to that of the Graham Greene character, the once famous French Catholic writer Morin, who, having lost his faith, continues to go to midnight mass because, he says, "I don't want to give scandal."

Someone suggested that if we were able to explain thoroughly the mysteries of religion, there'd be no room for faith. Julien Green says, "There is no faith without struggle." That does not seem to be the case with the Lama. The Lama makes no visible effort, attempts no explanations; he tells stories and follows his way, hoping that in the end he will be "free of the Wheel."

Kim's fat, pedantic companion, Hurree Babu: "How am I to fear the absolutely non-existent?"

Saturday

A very hot morning. My daughter Alice rescues a hedgehog from the pool. It had fallen in and was desperately swimming in circles. She carried it to a corner of the garden and allowed it to scuttle away, shivering.

A question of endings: I skip to the last pages of *Kim* for sheer pleasure. The end is an exuberant epiphany: Kim is made well and the Lama finds his river. His last gesture is to cross his hands and smile "as a man may who has won Salvation for himself and his beloved."

We read what we want to read, not what the author wrote. In *Don Quixote*, I'm not particularly interested in the world of chivalry but in the ethics of the hero, and in the curious friendship with Sancho. In *The Wind in the Willows*, I care far less about Mr. Toad than about Rat, Mole and Badger. In *Kim* I am not in the least interested in the Great Game, all that infantile spy-story stuff, but I'm enthralled by Kim's and the Lama's respective quests and by the brilliance of the depiction of a world I don't know.

Note: Literary travel is either a monologue or a dialogue, either the unraveling of one traveler's route (Ulysses, Pilgrim, Justine, Candide, the Wandering Jew) or two characters in mutual progression (Don Quixote and Sancho, Huckleberry Finn and Jim, Brother and Sister in search of the Blue Bird, Kim and his Lama).

Sunday

A second pair of mourning doves have taken up residence on the roof of the pigeon tower. They shimmer in the heat.

Summer in the garden carries implicitly all the year's changes: the winter branches before they sprouted spring leaves, the place where the fruit fell in the fall, the sequence of flowers. The regular coming and going of the seasons, the aging and death of friends, the crumbling of the walls of our house and the gnawing loss of my memory are a given, but they are also the confirmation (and the proof) of a constancy in things. Time is circular, these events say: after someone dies, I talk to someone else who remembers him, or wants to know something about him; we build up the garden wall with the stones that fell from the barn; what I no longer recall is there, somewhere, on one of the carefully numbered pages of one of my books. And I, of course, will disappear; the new wall, too, will fall away; the books will be scattered. But that of which we all form a part, a part however small, will stay on, fixed under the stars. And, as in the eye of a sculptor chiseling away at a stone, the whole will be all the more beautiful for our absence.

Monday

Kipling tells how one day his mother discovered a child's hand from the towers of silence dropped by a vulture in their garden in Bombay. Rohinton told me that such a thing isn't possible, because the vultures never stray that far from the towers.

A friend sends me a clipping from an English paper, with the heading "Housewife Kills 100 Magpies 'to Save Songbirds.'" To protect the birds she liked, the woman would trap magpies and then smash their heads against her garden wall.

Later

Kim's definition of love, when Father Victor asks him if he is fond of the Lama: "Of course I am fond of him. He was fond of me."

The Lama tells Kim stories "tracing with a finger in the dust." Like Christ, who "stooped down, and with his finger wrote in the ground, as if he heard them not."

Ana Becciú wrote this in *Ronda de noche*: "Love happens when we stroke a textured surface, when something is told with the hands or with the mouth. The mouth uses stories to stroke, causes scattered textures to appear, textures that can be read out loud. But almost no one knows how to read."

The perfect first paragraph of J. R. Ackerley's Indian journal, concerning the maharajah who employed him at his court: "He wanted someone to love him—His Highness, I mean; that was his real need, I think. He alleged other reasons, of course—an English private secretary, a tutor for his son; for he wasn't really a bit like the Roman Emperors, and had to make excuses."

Thursday

Title for a doctoral thesis: "The Novel as Obstacle Course."

The Lama believes that every obstacle in his way will be removed; Kim, that he himself is capable of either removing it or going around it. I read yesterday in Max Brod's biography that Kafka disliked Balzac and had noted with disapproval the motto Balzac had engraved on his walking stick: *"Je casse tout obstacle"* ("I shatter every obstacle"). Kafka then added his own motto: "Every obstacle shatters *me*."

Natural obstacles and political obstacles: Kipling obviously despises the white man who knows nothing of the land he lords over. The boy who is placed in charge of looking after Kim at the barracks beats him out of contempt and ignorance. The boy "styled all natives 'niggers'; yet servants and sweepers called him abominable names to his face, and, misled by their deferential attitude, he never understood. That somewhat consoled Kim for the beatings."

"There is no sin so great as ignorance," Creighton Sahib says later.

Friday

Years ago, Michael Ondaatje asked if I remembered the name of a certain British sergeant in *Kim*, because he wanted to use it in the novel he was writing.

"Read him slowly," says the English Patient to Hana, "you must read Kipling slowly. Watch carefully where the commas fall so you can discover the natural pauses. He is a writer who used pen and ink. He looked up from the page a lot."

On page 20 of my edition of *The English Patient* a French gun is mentioned, made in "Châttelrault." It should be "Châtellerault," a town famous for its arms factory, close to which I now, years later, live. Unfortunately, the greed of the local authorities has turned Châtellerault into a bleak commercial center, ignoring the beautiful sixteenth-century buildings (the house in which Descartes's father lived, for instance) and the elegant bridge over the Vienne, and laying out a huge parking lot, after cutting down all the trees.

Saturday

Kipling constantly turns the story to the point of view of the native characters: in *Kim* the British are outsiders attempting to rule, most of the time lost among the ancient alien cultures. He also understands that those over whom foreign rule is imposed (whether by Britain or by Rome) will always attempt to "drag down the State." In "A Pict Song" he wrote:

Rome never looks where she treads.
Always her heavy hooves fall
On our stomachs, our hearts or our heads;
And Rome never heeds when we bawl.

The contempt shown by the invader renders all collaboration suspect. Rabindranath Tagore, in a letter addressed to the Viceroy of India, relinquishing his knighthood after the Amritsar Massacre of 1919: "The universal agony of indignation roused in the hearts of our people has been ignored by our rulers . . . The time has come when badges of honour make our shame glaring in their incongruous context of humiliation, and I for my part wish to stand shorn of all special distinctions by the side of those of my countrymen who, for their so-called insignificance, are liable to suffer a degradation not fit for human beings."

In August, the newspapers seem devoid of news.

Monday

In my dreams, I'm never older than eighteen. The sixty-nine-year-old Mme du Deffand, writing to Horace Walpole: "I forget that I have lived, I am only thirteen."

I have the sense of having learned nothing since my late adolescence. The discoveries I made before are the ones that still hold; the rest seems trivial, unessential or at best a gloss. Kipling speaks of "the first rush of minds developed by sun and surroundings, as well as . . . the half-collapse that sets in at twenty-two or twenty-three."

Outside, the heat is fierce. Inside the house, because of the thick walls, it is wonderfully cool. I remember the same sensation in the hot Buenos Aires summers, lying in the almost dark, behind the grated iron shutters that allowed the air to blow through. Even sensations like these, felt now, are not new.

Adulthood defined by Kim's friend, the horse dealer Mahbud: "When I was fifteen, I had shot my man and begot my man."

Looking back at my adolescent readings, the essential, the most frightening question I remember is spoken "in a languid, sleepy voice" by the hookah-smoking Caterpillar in *Alice's Adventures in Wonderland*: "Who are *You*?" The active form of that question appears halfway through *Kim*: "What am I?" And then, a few chapters later: "Who is Kim-Kim-Kim?"

Kipling: "A very few white people, by many Asiatics, can throw themselves into amazement as it were by repeating their own names over and over again to themselves, letting the mind go free over speculation as to what is called identity. When one grows older, the power, usually, departs, but while it lasts it may descend upon a man at any moment."

Identity and place dissolve into what I remember or think I remember. As soon as I turn my head, it all becomes memory and changes accordingly. After the nightmarish tests in the house of

Lurgan Sahib, Kim must use all of his will to affirm the reality he knows ("It is there as it was there," he insists). Reality is that which Kim knows he sees (even if his eyes deny it), in all its kaleidoscopic strangeness.

A brilliant touch: the woman who stains Kim's skin to darken his colour "for protection" in the Great Game (thereby changing his outer identity) is blind.

Tuesday

Apart from my Bombay Edition, I have a number of Kipling books collected over time in many places. Two items I'm particularly fond of: a slim, badly tattered copy of *Under the Deodars*, N° 4 in Wheeler's Indian Railway Library, costing one rupee and published in Allahabad in 1888, when Kipling was twenty-three years old; and a red-bound pocket edition of *Stalky & Co.*, which the twenty-five-year-old Borges had bought upon his return to Buenos Aires in 1924, and which he gave me as a parting gift when I visited him in 1973.

A sort of autobiography could be written following the objects that have been given to me by friends. Here, in my writing room:

- a bronze statuette of Ganesh, elephant-headed god of beginnings, given to me by a long-lost friend after I received my first computer in 1984
- a glass pear that belonged to C.'s grandmother, which he gave me when we first met
- an Indian woven-metal pencil holder, a gift from Rohinton and Freny
- a Vietnamese stone box inlaid with signs I can't read, from Isabel Huggan, for my fiftieth birthday

- a paper column painted like a sky, from a set designed by Michael Levine for *Frühlings Erwachen*
- two pens—one a quill, the other a dipping pen—given to me by my two daughters
- a small clay snake made by Liza Detrick
- a leather book weight given to me by Barbara Moon
- a stone coaster that Lenny Fagin brought me back from India
- an incense dish made by Bodge Hall, which she gave me on the death of Rob Read, and which now carries stones from the Sybil's cave near Naples, from the Tessellated Pavement in Tasmania, from Colpoys Bay in Ontario, from a path in the Vosges Mountains and from the road outside my house in Calgary, as well as a ceramic bean given to me by Katherine and a Maya clay pendant that Ron Wright brought back for me from the Yucatán
- a small ebony arm, said to be part of the model followed in carving one of the gigantic Moors holding torches inside the Church of San Zaccaria in Venice
- a box holding postcards, hand-painted by the owner of the *tabac* across from our flat in the Alsatian village of Sélestat, where I spent a year researching in the humanist library

In his autobiography, Kipling lists the objects he keeps on his writing desk. "Like most men who ply one trade in one place for any while, I always kept certain gadgets on my work-table, which was ten feet long from North to South and badly congested. One was a long, lacquer, canoe-shaped pen-tray full of brushes and dead 'fountains'; a wooden box held clips and bands; another, a tin one, pins; yet another, a bottle-slider, kept all manner of unneeded essentials from emery-paper to small screwdrivers; a paper-weight, said to have been Warren Hastings'; a tiny, weighted fur-seal and a leather crocodile sat on some of the papers; an inky foot-rule and a Father of Penwipers which a much-loved housemaid of ours presented yearly, made up the main-guard of these little fetishes."

Thursday

A letter with a return address I don't recognize, forwarded by my American publisher. Out of nowhere, someone whose name now means nothing to me writes to say that we met when I was eleven or twelve years old and that something I did then has stayed with him all these years. I wonder at the long, late results of things I have forgotten doing or saying—unimportant, casual things.

Half an hour later, I pick up *Kim* where I left off reading yesterday and find these words spoken by the Lama: "Thou hast loosed an Act upon the world, and as a stone thrown into a pool so spread the consequences thou canst not tell how far."

Saturday

The last day of the month.

In Spanish the word for "waiting," *espera*, shares the same root as "hope," *esperanza*. Gide in his *Journal* says this: "*Sala de espera*. What a beautiful language, one that confuses waiting with hope!"

The end of *Kim* is about waiting, and finding that one has achieved what one has been striving for almost without knowing it. The Lama's final vision is like that of Saint Benedict of Nursia, who, sometime in the sixth century, looked up from his prayers and saw in the darkness outside his window that "the whole world appeared to be gathered into one sunbeam and thus brought before his eyes."

The last line in Patrick White's *The Tree of Man*: "So that, in the end, there was no end."

SEPTEMBER

Saturday

C. accompanies our neighbor, Mme H., to the cemetery of our village, to look for the tomb of the marquis who lived in the castle here during her childhood. She is seventy-seven years old and has trouble keeping her balance when walking. The cemetery is a small enclosure, transferred to the outskirts of the village during the eighteenth century. When they find the mausoleum, C. helps her descend the narrow stairs and switches on a flashlight to help her read the dates. His death is later than she thought. *"Mon dernier marquis!"* she sighs.

What I remember most of Chateaubriand's *Memoirs from Beyond the Grave* is not his mourning for the passing of the French aristocracy but the sustained elegiac tone. And the vastness. The two volumes of *La Pléiade* are daunting; to feel more comfortable amidst two thousand pages, I refer to my penciled notes at the back.

I always write in my books. When I reread them, most of the time I can't imagine why I thought a certain passage worth underlining, or what I meant by a certain comment. Yesterday I came across a copy of Victor Segalen's *René Leys* dated Trieste, 1978. I don't remember ever being in Trieste.

Encouraged by Mme Récamier to write his memoirs, Chateaubriand sets out to cover almost an entire century, from his birth in 1768 to 1841, barely seven years before his death. His is a daunting project: to recall his childhood in Saint-Malo, his adolescence in Cobourg, his military career in Paris and his witnessing of the French Revolution, his voyage to the New World, his painful exile in England, his early sympathy for Napoleon's ambitions, his later disenchantment with the emperor and his final role as Foreign Affairs minister under the Bourbons. Above all, his attempt to establish possession over the years gone by.

Few autobiographers allow time itself to hold the foreground; most are too fascinated by the progress of their own fond person. To read Chateaubriand is to witness the subjective and yet comprehensive unfolding of a society's change: of customs, prospects, ethics, conventions. He stands (as in the famous portrait by Girodet) on the farther shore, looking at the aristocratic trappings that have been taken from him, and I can't sympathize with that loss. But at the same time he tells of a deeper loss due to age, to experience, to a twist in desire, and to this loss I feel intimately close. In his youth, he recalls, he was "troubled by a longing for happiness"; now, in his old age, he quietly observes "the reflections of a dawn whose sun I will not see rise."

Douglas LePan, writing to me in the fall of 1995, shortly before his death, had this to say: "I regard it as slightly unfair that I must be preparing to take my leave at just the moment when the game here is beginning to become interesting."

I read Chateaubriand as my contemporary.

Tuesday

I have a literary interest in religions. I have no formal training in any of them, so my religious practice (or, rather, lack of it) is piecemeal and haphazard. Yehuda Elberg gave me, a few years ago, an eighteenth-century silver mezuzah, which I fixed onto the right-hand doorpost of my writing room, as the injunction in Deuteronomy commands. Following tradition, I placed it diagonally, a compromise reached between those medieval Talmudists who argued for the horizontal position, and those who preferred the vertical.

I read somewhere of a debate on whether Jewish prison cells should carry a mezuzah, since only permanent residences require one and it is hoped that residence in a prison is not permanent. The scripture inside the mezuzah promises, among other things, rain in due season: "the first rain and the latter rain, that thou mayest gather in thy corn, and thy wine, and thine oil." In my case, I take these to be metaphors for writing.

Chateaubriand, wondering whether God is satisfied with one's work as with one's life, succinctly asks, "Is a book enough for God?" I should hope so.

Wednesday

A year ago today, my daughter Alice called me from Ottawa to tell me the unbelievable news that a plane had crashed into the World Trade Center. Throughout the day she called back, sobbing, with updates. She was alone in her apartment and needed to share the horror. Since I didn't have a television set, I listened to the radio. Not seeing the images allowed me room, I believe, for reflection while the carnage was being described. The hatred explicit in the act seemed overwhelming. How far does someone need to be pushed to breed such hatred of the Other?

The Other, defined in two lines by Browning that have troubled me since school:

> I never saw a brute I hated so;
> He must be wicked to deserve such pain.

The nineteenth century called terrorists Nihilists, those who care for nothing. They are not afraid of dying; their slogan is the one chanted by the fascists during the Spanish Civil War: *¡Viva la muerte!*

That evening, before going to sleep, I opened Chateaubriand and read how he confesses that the revolution would have caught him up in its flow, had he not seen the first head carried at the end of a pike. And then I came upon this: "Murder will never be in my eyes an object of admiration and an argument for freedom; I know nothing more servile, more despicable, more cowardly, more narrow-minded than a terrorist."

Thursday

On the train, a week ago, I read Thomas Harris's sequel to *The Silence of the Lambs*. The hero-monster with no purpose in life except his own satisfaction: has that character been created at any other time in history? Hannibal Lecter is our egotistical role, and ours a society in which an acceptable image of revenge is literally eating your enemy's brains out. How can we then complain of other people's madness?

I mention this on the phone to Katherine, who says that I always exaggerate.

Afternoon

The West recognizes the Other only to better despise it, and is then astonished at the answer reflected back. Ferdinando Camon once said to Primo Levi, "There is something in Christian culture that recommends relations with 'the Other' with the sole purpose of achieving his conversion . . . The fate of 'the Other' is considered as nothing compared to his conversion. If you look into this assertion, at the end of a certain time you can see extermination."

The old truisms still hold: that violence breeds violence; that all power is abusive; that fanaticism of any kind is the enemy of reason; that propaganda is propaganda even when it purports to rally us against iniquity; that war is never glorious except in the eyes of the victors, who believe that God is on the side of the big battalions.

Maybe this is why we read, and why in moments of darkness we return to books: to find words for what we already know.

Chateaubriand: "We live only by means of style."

The horror felt at acts such as those of last year echoes back throughout history: the horror of the Arabs at the brutality of the first Crusaders; the Incas disbelieving that anything human could be as sanguinary as the hordes of Pizarro; the Tasmanian aborigines unable to put into words (their language did not possess the terms) the brutishness of the European settlers.

History, in our eyes, seems to take place through comparisons.

A few days after the tragedy, I heard of someone who had been trapped that morning inside a bookstore close to the World Trade Center. Since there was nothing to do but wait for the dust to settle, he kept on browsing through the books, in the midst of the sirens and the screams. Chateaubriand notes that, during the chaos of the French Revolution, a Breton poet just arrived in Paris asked to be taken on a tour of Versailles. "There are people," Chateaubriand comments, "who, while empires collapse, visit fountains and gardens."

Friday

In 1930 André Breton outrageously suggested that "the simplest Surrealist act consists of dashing down into the street, pistol in hand, and firing blindly, as fast as you can pull the trigger, into the crowd." He meant the action to exist only in the sphere of the unrestrained imagination. He was writing about literature; reality co-opted his writing.

I meet Mavis Gallant at La Rotonde for coffee. She tells me how struck she was last year by the French need to show sympathy for America, and how anyone with the slightest "American" accent (Canadian, Australian or whatever) received condolences; she felt obliged to accept them graciously. A friend of hers went into a shop in Paris and, having shown herself by her accent to be "American," was immediately surrounded by well-wishers and sympathizers, only to discover, minutes later, that her credit card had been pinched.

Tuesday

In his memoir on Torquato Tasso, Chateaubriand notes how convinced the poet was of a numinous presence in the world. One day, sitting by the fire, he saw a ray of sun enter through a window and remarked, *"Ecco l'amico spirito che cortesemente è venuto favellarmi."* ("Here's the friendly spirit that has so politely come to converse with me.")

A few months ago, C. tried to save a magnolia tree that we had to remove when we decided to rebuild the collapsing barn in order to lodge the library. He replanted it and hopes it will survive. The tree looks terribly frail, cut back and thin. Chateaubriand begins his *Memoirs* with a few trees he has planted in his garden in Aulnay, so small that he would cast them into shadow when he stood "between them and the sun."

Mavis sent a card with something she had forgotten to tell me—how someone described the people throwing themselves out of the World Trade Center: "They looked like commas in the sky."

Thursday

All day it has been sunny. There are bees flying very low, buzzing around my ankles in the grass. I feel exhausted by the news (the invention of the "war on terrorism," the justifications for invading Iraq) on our newly acquired television, and by the recapitulations of last year's events.

We create climates of hatred. During the military dictatorship in Argentina, the loathing and fear felt toward anyone in uniform were palpable. I've felt that on different occasions, when visiting Barbados, Iraq, Jerusalem.

Maybe our rulers and our gods must be made to look angry. Julien Green says that, in the eighteenth century in Scotland, the word "wrath" kept coming up so frequently in the pulpit that a certain printer of sermons, having exhausted his provision of *W*s, was forced to use two *V*s instead.

Our god is the god of fairy tales, setting tests for his three sons, each of whom believes himself to be the best-loved, though none is ever truly "the chosen one."

In Georges Courteline's *Les Balances*:

> So tell me, you were mentioning God a while ago. Do you know him?
>
> Yes and no. I know him in that I've heard him mentioned, but we're not on such intimate terms that we'd play billiards together.

Chateaubriand assumes that a world has come to an end and that he, a shadow among shadows, will write down what he recalls of its destruction. Perhaps that is all we do: remember. Does all this dredging up of images and words serve a purpose? "The recollections that awaken in my memory overwhelm me with their power and their volume. And yet, what are they for the rest of the world?"

Doris Lessing, commenting on September 11: "Americans felt that they had lost Paradise. They never asked themselves why they thought they had the right to be there in the first place."

David Wojnarowicz, from "In the Shadow of the American Dream: Soon All This Will Be Picturesque Ruins," written in 1991: "Americans can't deal with death unless they own it."

The ancient Anglo-Saxons allowed Roman buildings to crumble and then wrote elegies to the ruins. Other examples? The correspondence of the illustrious French women of the eighteenth century; the English detective novel of the golden age; Joseph Roth and Sandor Marai; the novels and stories of Mavis Gallant; the *Pillow Book of Sei Shonagon* . . . all these attempts to recapture the past have a deep elegiac quality.

For Chateaubriand, the world we see is *already* memory: of things fleeting, ephemeral, gone and yet unwilling to relinquish us entirely. The past will not go away; what we are experiencing exists only in the moment that goes by.

Chateaubriand tells the story of his sister's spiritual director, a certain M. Livoret, who on the night of his appointment was visited for the first time by the apparition of a certain Count of Châteaubourg. The ghost pursued him everywhere: indoors, in the forests, in the fields. One day, unable to bear it any longer,

M. Livoret turned to the ghost and said, "Monsieur de Châteaubourg, please leave me," to which the ghost answered, "No."

For us it is the present that is constant; we refuse to let it go. Newscasters take for granted a public infected with forgetfulness, unable to recall what occurred moments earlier; a public in need of the constant ghost of "the event." Is this our attempt to eliminate mortality? Brief flashes, repetition, a sense of immediacy; we are offered something like a never-ending moment that allows no distance in time or space.

Another definition of Hell: the eternal reenactment of a deed purged of any possibility of passing.

Chateaubriand: "One thing humbles me: memory is often a quality associated with foolishness; usually it belongs to slow-witted souls whom it renders even slower because of the baggage it loads upon them. And yet, what would we be without memory? We would forget our friendships, our loves, our pleasures, our business; genius would be unable to collect its thoughts; the most affectionate of hearts would lose its tenderness if it did not remember; our existence would be reduced to the successive moments of an endlessly flowing present. There would be no past."

The last word in the *Memoirs* is "eternity."

Friday

A village squabble, or *querelle de clocher*. Our mayor has decided to install mechanical bells in the church tower, since the old, hand-rung ones were riddled with bullets fired years ago by a drunken hunter. Several of the villagers gather outside the church door to discuss at what time the bells should start and stop ringing. They quickly vote down the traditional custom of ringing twice every hour, begun so that whoever has not started counting from the first toll may be able to start his count again. An ex-gendarme, who lives at the far end of the village and can therefore barely hear the bells, argues that they should begin with the angelus at six, and end with the angelus twelve hours later. Several others, who live close to the church, disagree because they don't want to be woken up so early in the morning. The argument becomes heated. Finally, exasperated, my neighbor, a longtime socialist brought up on the secular legislation imposed by the French Revolution (which Chateaubriand so deeply regretted) blurts:

> "You know what you can do with your angelus? You can go stuff it up your . . . !"
>
> To which the ex-gendarme, drawing himself up very straight and very stiff, replies:
>
> "Monsieur, if we lose the angelus, we lose France!"

An infinite number of tiny moments of bliss, almost always unexpected, very fleeting, unremarkable. The sight of the full moon outside the window, the taste of a certain apricot jam, the sudden pressure of a hand, a line by Stevenson in *Kidnapped*: "I've a grand memory for forgetting . . ."

The weight of happiness: Chateaubriand says that he has always gained strength from adversity. "If ever happiness had seized me in its arms, I would have suffocated."

And yet not everything he recalls is adversity. He describes how, as a child, he lusted after Dido in the *Aeneid* and translated

Lucretius's *Aeneadum genitrix, hominum divumque voluptas* ("Mother of Aeneas's sons, voluptuous delight of men and gods") with such ardour that his teacher tore the poem from his hands and set him to study Greek roots.

Chateaubriand's childhood reading: "I would steal small candle-ends in the chapel to read at night the seductive descriptions of the troubles of the soul." I, too, remember reading, throughout a wonderfully long summer, all sorts of books in which I unexpectedly found an erotic apprenticeship, under the cool sheets, my skin hot from the sun, a flashlight shining its light on the page, driven by the unwillingness to fall asleep and let the story break off.

Beckford, at the beginning of *Vathek*: "He did not think, with the Caliph Omar ben Abdalaziz, that it was necessary to make a hell of this world to enjoy paradise in the next."

Saturday

Pouring rain that steams on the hot earth.

Today we gave the son of the previous owners of our house an ancient stone capital we dug up during the renovations, so that he would have a piece of his childhood space in the new house he is building.

Chateaubriand: "The chain of historical events, the destiny of men, the destruction of empires, the designs of Providence, presented themselves in my memory as recollections of my own fate: after having explored lifeless ruins, I was called upon to witness the spectacle of ruins that were still alive."

For Chateaubriand, the very notion of aristocracy is worthy of respect. In 1847, thirteen years after Chateaubriand's *Memoirs* had been completed, Victor Hugo gave an example of how the nineteenth century now expressed its respect for aristocracy: "The Prince of Wales, in 1860, visits Canada and the United States. The acrobat Blondin, in a letter to New York's *Evening Post*, suggests that, in order to add to the solemnity of the prince's entrance into the Union, he will without charge convey His Royal Highness in a wheelbarrow on a tightrope across Niagara Falls."

Later

Memoirs from Beyond the Grave is, among other things, a colossal anthology of brief lives, the portrait of a man acting as his own and his contemporaries' Boswell.

Some examples:

- Shortly before the Revolution, Chateaubriand is introduced to the queen: "Casting her eyes on me with a smile, she greeted me in the same charming style with which she had done so the day of my presentation. I will not forget that look, which was to be extinguished so soon after. Marie-Antoinette, smiling, displayed so perfectly the shape of her mouth that the memory of that smile (frightful thought!) allowed me to recognize the jaw of that daughter of kings, when the head of the unfortunate lady was discovered during the exhumations in 1815."
- Upon arriving in the United States, Chateaubriand is greeted by a young black slave selling corn cakes, chick-

ens, eggs and milk. After paying her, he gives her his silken handkerchief and notes, "It was a slave who welcomed me to the land of freedom."

- At the death of Pope Clement XII, the Cardinal Chamberlain, according to protocol, knocked two or three times on His Eminence's forehead, calling him by his name, to make sure that he was dead. After describing this scene, Chateaubriand comments, "What would he have said if Clement XII had answered him, from the depths of eternity, 'Well? What do you want?'"

Why do I enjoy this intimacy with Chateaubriand, privileged witness of a certain time and place? Above all, because of the sense of sharing secret stories, gossiping about things hidden and revealing. Proust to Philippe Soupault: "You know, I'm a bit of a concierge."

Chateaubriand on journal-keeping and the need to write down one's impressions immediately: "Our existence is so fleeting that if we don't record the events of the morning in the evening, the work will weigh us down and we will no longer have the time to bring it up to date. This doesn't prevent us from wasting our years, from throwing to the wind those hours that are for us the seeds of eternity."

He is also shameless in his literary intentions. History, yes, but above all it must suit his elegant imagination. He says that he needed "a useful purpose" for his voyage across the Atlantic, so he "proposed to discover the Northwest Passage." "This project," he says, "was not unrelated to my poetic nature."

Sunday

The American government announces in the press that it does indeed possess a "Department of Disinformation." I can't decide what is more outrageous: the existence of such a department, or the acknowledgment of its existence.

Chateaubriand, commenting on the lies contained in a political speech by Talleyrand, who had served as Foreign Affairs minister under Louis XVIII: "There are absences of memory, or lies, that frighten; you open your ears, you rub your eyes, not knowing whether you are deceived by wakefulness or by sleep . . . You can't tell whether this man has perhaps received from nature such authority that he has the power to re-create or annihilate truth."

Monday

This promises to be a quiet week at home. There are writers I can read in the midst of a racket, but I need quiet to sit down with Chateaubriand; otherwise I miss too much of the tone under the style.

Much of Chateaubriand's *Memoirs* is concerned with Napoleon, first as a possible heroic figure, then as a tyrant. His chronicle of disillusionment reminds me of other similar attachments and disattachments: Gide and Stalin, Sontag and Castro . . .

A reproach that sounds self-intended: "All that the world perceives in Napoleon are his victories."

Chateaubriand's account of Napoleon's tyranny is applicable to almost any other dictatorship: "Those who were persecuted dreaded seeing their friends, for fear of compromising them; their friends dared not visit them, for fear of provoking even heavier persecution. The unfortunate outlaw, become a pariah, cut off from human company, remained in the quarantine of the despot's hatred. Welcomed as long as your freedom of opinion remained secret, everything was withdrawn as soon as it became known; nothing was left to keep you company but the authorities spying on your relationships, on what you had to say, on your correspondence, on your dealings with others. Such were those days of happiness and freedom."

Chateaubriand as European. In 1934 Thomas Mann, recalling a meeting with his old mentor, the German publisher Sammi Fischer, noted in his journal an observation made by Fischer about a mutual acquaintance:

> "He is no European," he said, shaking his head.
>
> "No European, Herr Fischer? Why ever not?"
>
> "He understands nothing of the great humane ideas."

Borges reviewing James Whale's 1937 film *The Road Back*: "Mere pacifism is not enough. War is an ancient passion that tempts men with ascetic and mortal charms. To abolish war, another passion must be opposed to it. Perhaps that of the *good European*—Leibniz, Voltaire, Goethe, Arnold, Renan, Shaw, Russell, Unamuno, T. S. Eliot—who knows himself heir and successor of all countries. There is in Europe a surfeit of mere Germans or mere Irish; what is lacking is Europeans."

Tuesday

Now the church bells begin to ring at eight, too late to be of any use as an alarm clock.

My son, Rupert, is here on a visit. We talk about the politics of absolute power and I read him these lines by Chateaubriand on Napoleon: "To become disgusted with conquerors, it would be necessary to know all the evils they cause; it would be necessary to witness the indifference with which the most innocent creatures are sacrificed to them in a corner of the world on which they have never set foot."

Rupert tells me that he despairs of being able to remain true to his ethics in a world he perceives as corrupted, run by myriad corporate Napoleons. How to know which of our acts are compromises, which are strategies for survival, which are sellouts? The tactics of greed (Napoleon's desire to own *everything*, for instance) are astonishing; they have no limits, not even those of their own destruction.

At dinner, we recall reading Oscar Wilde's children's stories written when he was seven or eight, in Toronto. I fetch a copy of the book and read Wilde's description of a dream in "The Young King." Avarice and Death watch a multitude of men toiling in the mud. "They are my servants," says Avarice, holding in her palm three grains of corn. Death proposes a bargain: for one grain of corn, she will leave the men alone. Avarice refuses, and Death kills a third of them. Three times the offer is made and three times it is refused. In the end, no man is left alive.

Wednesday

More rain, but it does not feel any cooler. It's late at night. I listen to the 1893 version of Fauré's *Requiem*, not the showy, loud version of 1900, but the version he imagined before it was rewritten for a full orchestra. Fauré had composed an even earlier version in 1887 ("for the pleasure of it," he said), after the death of both his parents. That first version has no reference to the Day of Judgment, and the few strings mostly double the organ. Then, six years later, in January, he added two baritone pieces: the "Offertorium" and the "Libera me." In this unostentatious version the composer disappears; only the listener remains present. In the "Introitus," for instance, what we hear is ourselves, our own voice calling "from the depths." Fauré is offstage, invisible. Reading *Memoirs from Beyond the Grave*, I forget that it is Chateaubriand, not I, who is mourning.

Thursday

In the end, says Chateaubriand, nothing perishes. "My faithfulness towards the memory of my dead friends should lend confidence to those friends who are left to me: nothing for me steps down into the shadow; everything I once knew lives all around me. According to the Indian doctrine, death, when it touches us, does not destroy us; it merely renders us invisible."

Cocteau, in his diary: "Invisibility seems to me the condition of elegance."

❧ OCTOBER ❧

Saturday

I'm on a book tour in Germany, reading in a different city every day. It's as if it were still summer: the outdoor terraces are open, the geraniums are in full bloom in the window boxes everywhere.

I'm in Münster today. I'm sitting at an outdoor café on a cobbled pedestrian street, reading Conan Doyle's *The Sign of Four*, close to a monument to the Holocaust showing a Jewish woman on her knees, cleaning the pavement with a toothbrush. I order a cup of ice cream and red-fruit compote (*Rote Grütze*). The waitress, an East German woman in an embroidered white apron, trips against a chair and the cup falls on the stones. Catching the supervisor's eye, she apologizes in a panic and goes down on all fours to clean up the red mess.

In Münster Cathedral, bombed by the Allies, a stone from Coventry Cathedral, "destroyed 4 Nov. 1940," and the notice "Forgiving one another as God in Christ forgave you." I find in this an almost malicious irony, with a feeling of boasting on either side.

George Meredith in *Modern Love*:

> 'Tis morning: but no morning can restore
> What we have forfeited. I see no sin:
> The wrong is mixed. In tragic life, God wot,
> No villain need be! Passions spin the plot:
> We are betrayed by what is false within.

Sunday

Last Thursday, in Munich, at the Literaturhaus, I saw an exhibition of photographs of actors taken from many different performances; the ensemble of faces creates a new performance. The different arrangement of facts forms a new pattern, a new story, a new theory (if this were a detective story) of what really happened.

In a detective story, often the assumption is that anyone can be the murderer.

This morning, crossing the country by train: the wonderful German forests, so like the pictures in my fairy-tale books. Then the thought: through these forests, hunted prisoners ran.

Afternoon

Berlin. Most German cities have an asepticized look that other cities (London, for instance) never have. This is, no doubt, due to the eye of the outsider, who, like Watson, never sees beyond appearances. This week, everywhere I go, I see a series of posters announcing a new campaign against drugs, and even the addicts depicted on the posters look scrubbed and neat.

In my late teens and early twenties I believed that, at any moment, someone would see through my appearance and discover all my secrets. I was afraid that, under the right scrutiny, even my thoughts would not remain hidden for long, and that the keen observer, like a shrewd detective, would know that I was guilty of all sorts of forbidden things.

The first time I took LSD was in a cheap London hotel with three other people, one of them our high school monitor from Buenos Aires. This was 1969 or 1970; I was twenty one or twenty-two, and I had no definable expectations about the experience to come. I had read Huxley and Castaneda, but (as so often in those days) found it impossible to imagine that the literary experience of others might convincingly match my own. What took place on the page unfolded in a separate time, to which, yes, I had access, but as to a parallel universe, truer and more lasting than the one ruled by concerns of money, food, health, sex and the heart. So when the monitor suggested we all take the tiny blue pills he had with him, I said yes, of course, without any inclination to compare what was to come with what I had read a long time ago.

But if the obvious books were not on my mind at the time, others fell open unbidden. Perhaps the distribution of comfit-like pills, the round dodo eyes of my monitor, the street name of the hotel (Lewis), the contradictory sensation of falling and floating, made me think of another fall and of other adventures, and I started scribbling in a large blue onion-paper notepad thoughts about *Alice's Adventures in Wonderland* that appeared momentous then, and now read as banal, when not incomprehensible. On the seventh page, after noting something illegible about ceilings and the rhythm of my lungs, I wrote, as a sudden illumination with no reference to Alice, *THE SIGN OF 4!!!* in large block letters.

I first read the Sherlock Holmes stories in a rented summer house in Mar del Plata, on the Atlantic coast south of Buenos Aires, one book after another, unable to stop. I'm not certain what charmed me then: not the plots, since *El Séptimo Círulo*, the detective series edited by Borges and Bioy Casares, offered far more intriguing puzzles and original solutions; not the words, which seemed to me far less enchanting than those of Stevenson or Kipling. Perhaps it was what Chesterton calls "the thread of irony which runs through all the solemn impossibilities of the narrative," which he thought turned the Holmes stories into "a really brilliant addition to the great literature of nonsense." Perhaps it was the chilly yet reassuring presence of a place that was to become haunted by my daydreams.

For me, no German city (neither Döblin's Berlin nor Thomas Mann's Lübeck) ever had the reality of Conan Doyle's London: the gaslit rooms in Baker Street, the evil winding streets, the genteel foggy squares. Years later I traveled to London, convinced that I would find that memorable geography. My first shilling-metered bed-sitter above a fish-and-chips shop disabused me.

I can't remember my reaction to the discovery that Sherlock Holmes was a cocaine addict. The opening paragraph of *The Sign of Four*, describing the Master taking the bottle "from the corner of the mantelpiece" and the hypodermic syringe "from its neat morocco case," and then, "with his long, white, nervous fingers" adjusting the "delicate needle" and rolling back "his left shirt-cuff" and finally thrusting "the sharp point home"—all this in the presence of Doctor Watson—gripped me without scandal. (I was far more scandalized by the intrusion of the demonic ghostly dog in *The Hound of the Baskervilles*, for instance.) And yet later, in a far different London than the one I thought I loved, enjoying my first chemical hallucinations, I remembered that scene above all. Holmes's comment to Watson's criticism—"I suppose that its influence is physically a bad one. I find it, however, so transcendingly stimulating and clarifying to the mind that its secondary action is a matter of small moment"—rang true. Three more times I took LSD. Then I stopped, not for cautionary reasons but because I felt the experience would simply repeat itself, like watching the same film again, for the fourth time.

Graham Greene, on the opening paragraph of *The Sign of Four*: "What popular author today could so abruptly introduce his hero as a drug addict without protest from his public? It is only in one direction that we have become a permissive society."

Tomorrow I leave for France.

Monday

I find it easy to read, difficult to write in trains.

This morning, outside the window of the train on my way home, a short, almost imperceptible snowstorm. In the Book of Common Prayer: "He giveth snow like wool." And "A joyful and pleasant thing it is to be thankful." I make a mental list of descriptions of snow in books I've read and think that, since there are so many, they would not coincide with those of another reader.

Later

Holmes as tragic hero, feeling trapped in a stifling world, suffering from the pain of existence. Instances of *Weltschmerz*.

HOLMES: I cannot live without brainwork. What else is there to live for? Stand at the window here. Was there ever such a dreary, dismal, unprofitable world? See how the yellow fog swirls down the street and drifts across the dun-coloured houses. What could be more hopelessly prosaic and material? What is the use of having powers, doctor, when one has no field upon which to exert them?

FAUST: God, how these walls still cramp my soul,
This cursèd, stifling prison-hole . . .
And can you still ask why your heart
Is pent and pining in your breast,
Why you obscurely ache and smart,
Robbed of all energy and zest?
For here you sit, surrounded not
By living Nature, not as when
God made us, but by reek and rot
And mouldering bones of beasts and men.
(David Luke's translation)

PRUFROCK: The yellow fog that rubs its back upon the windowpanes,

> The yellow smoke that rubs its muzzle on the windowpanes
> Licked its tongue into the corners of the evening . . .

What is *The Sign of Four* about? The search for balance as a cure for ennui. Balance is, perhaps, the main theme of every detective story. Revenge (a form of balance). Cause and consequence (another). Justice (another).

P. D. James: "What the detective story is about is not murder but the restoration of order."

Tuesday

Back home. The cat who has decided to take up residence here seems offended that I have left her that long, and walks away when I approach her. I leave the door of the library open to tempt her to come in.

Long ago I discovered a remarkable book by a certain Samuel Rosenberg, *Naked Is the Best Disguise.* Rosenberg worked as a literary consultant for major motion-picture studios, which hired him when they were sued for plagiarism. His job was "to analyze the embattled scripts, and when the resemblances between 'theirs' and 'ours' were too close for comfort, I tried to get my employers off the litigious hook by searching for common literary ancestors of both properties." Using the Holmes canon as his starting point, Rosenberg manages to link Nietzsche, Melville, Mary Shelley, Boccaccio, Racine, Flaubert and many others to the Sherlockian saga. Rosenberg sees the character of Thaddeus Sholto, in *The Sign of Four*, as a parody or portrait of Oscar Wilde, including the Habsburg lip. (In 1889, Wilde and Conan Doyle met at a dinner given by the American representative of *Lippincott's Magazine*. As a result, both men became contributors: Wilde with *The Picture of Dorian Gray* and Conan Doyle with Sholto's adventure.)

Coincidences:

- Conan Doyle's description of Thaddeus Sholto: "Nature had given him a pendulous lip, and a too visible line of yellow and irregular teeth, which he strove feebly to conceal by constantly passing his hand over the lower part of his face. In spite of his obtrusive baldness, he gave the impression of youth."
- Hesketh Pearson's description of Wilde: He "had thick, purple-tinged sensual lips, uneven discoloured teeth . . . it was noticed that when talking he frequently put a bent finger over his mouth which showed that he was conscious of his unattractive teeth."

Says Chesterton: "We have to consider not only what is improbable, but what is probable; and especially the coincidences that are overwhelmingly probable."

Thursday

Spent yesterday rearranging the detective fiction. We've put it up in the guest bedroom, now to be known as the Murder Room.

The Sign of Four: The phrase as it appears in the story is "the sign of *the* four," but only someone deaf to cadence would use it in a title, as Conan Doyle did in *Lippincott's Magazine* in February 1890. Someone or something told him to drop the second "the" when the story was published in book form.

List of my favorite detective novels:

- Nicholas Blake, *The Beast Must Die*
- Reginald Hill, *Bones and Silence*
- Ruth Rendell, *A Judgement in Stone*
- Agatha Christie, *The Murder of Roger Ackroyd*
- John Dickson Carr, *The Black Spectacles*
- Marco Denevi, *Rosaura a las diez*
- Margaret Millar, *How Like an Angel*
- Fruttero & Lucentini, *La Donna della domenica*
- James Cain, *Mildred Pierce*
- Philip Kerr, *A Philosophical Investigation*
- Dorothy L. Sayers, *Gaudy Night*
- Leo Perutz, *The Master of the Day of Judgement*
- John Franklin Bardin, *Devil Take the Blue-Tail Fly*
- Ellery Queen, *The Tragedy of X*
- Anthony Berkeley, *Trial and Error*
- Sébastien Japrisot, *Compartiment tueur*
- James McClure, *The Steam Pig*
- Raymond Postgate, *Verdict of Twelve*
- Georges Simenon, *Les fiançailles de Monsieur Hire*
- Patrick Quentin, *My Son the Murderer*
- Chester Himes, *Cotton Comes to Harlem*

Friday

We hear this morning that our postwoman's husband has committed suicide. It suddenly seems obscene to be entertained by brutal deaths in fiction.

Sunday

At the end of Chapter 6, Holmes quotes (in German) a line from Goethe (*Faust*, I): *"Wir sind gewohnt dass die Menschen verhöhnen was sie nicht verstehen."* ("We are accustomed that men will mock what they don't understand.") The detective story elicits the possibility of mockery but at the same time prohibits it; the reader is already converted to the faith, wants *not* to know, wants to be deceived in order to be better entertained.

Questions that in themselves delight: Why and how has this happened? Who is responsible? What plan lies behind this confusion of facts? The reader assumes the role of a detached Job, in which sentiment is a mere adornment or distraction. Aware of this, Holmes accuses Watson of introducing sentiment in his account of the puzzle: "You have attempted to tinge it with romanticism, which produces the same effect as if you worked a love-story or an elopement into the fifth proposition of Euclid."

And yet, as one of the characters in the novel remarks, *The Sign of Four* "is a romance!" She sums it up: "An injured lady, half a million in treasure, a black cannibal, and a wooden-legged ruffian. They take the place of the conventional dragon or wicked earl . . ."

To plot the adventures of his hero, Conan Doyle builds on the social conventions of his age. Since in the classic detective story nothing must seem unexpected except that which is deliberately put forward as unconventional, the adventures must follow society's expected behaviour according to class, sex, etc. and implied responsibilities, codes of honor and such among "ladies and gentlemen" and what Holmes calls "people of that sort." One shudders to read the condescending tone of the hero toward his "lesser" fellow human beings. Observing workers emerging from the dockyards after their day is over, Holmes comments, "Dirty-looking rascals, but I suppose every one has some little immortal spark concealed about him. You would not think it, to look at them."

"A historian of the future will probably turn, not to blue books or statistics, but to detective stories if he wishes to study the manners of our age," wrote C. H. B. Kitchin some forty years later.

Note: As an example of this reliance on social conventions, the message sent to Mary Morstan (the damsel in distress who is to become Watson's wife): "Be at the third pillar from the left outside the Lyceum Theatre tonight at seven o'clock. If you are distrustful, bring two friends. You are a wronged woman, and shall have justice. Do not bring police. If you do, all will be in vain. Your unknown friend." Even here, the note requires the happy coincidence of allowing for *two* friends (not just one) in order for both Holmes and Watson to be able to accompany the lady without breaking the code of honor. (Later Miss Morstan will have to give her word to the "unknown friend" that "neither of your companions is a police-officer." As she is a lady, her word, of course, suffices.)

Monday

Tender scenes of male friendship in Conan Doyle's staunchly macho world. Holmes to Watson: "Lie down there on the sofa and see if I can put you to sleep." He then takes up his violin from the corner, while Watson stretches himself out. "I have a vague remembrance," Watson says, "of his gaunt limbs, his earnest face, and the rise and fall of his bow. Then I seemed to be floated peacefully away upon a soft sea of sound, until I found myself in dreamland, with the sweet face of Mary Morstan looking down upon me."

That "sweet face of Mary Morstan" seems tagged on, as a precautionary afterthought.

Tuesday

Last Sunday, at the flea market in Chinon, I found a first edition of Boris Vian's *L'écume des jours.*

It occurs to me that *L'écume des jours* depicts a French version of the Holmes-Watson relationship in the characters of Colin and his friend Chick. Holmes's demand that there be no vagueness in the narrative is taken literally in this surrealist fantasy. So if someone says, *"Poussez le feu"* (literally, "push the fire"), he can add *"et, sur l'espace ainsi gagné . . ."* ("and, in the newly gained space . . ."); if someone is *"planté là"* ("rooted there"), he will indeed sprout roots.

Vian even lends exact words to Holmes's *Weltschmerz*: "I spend my brightest hours darkening them because light bothers me."

Because of phrases like this one, I understand why Cortázar told the poet Alejandra Pizarnik that, after finishing *L'écume des jours*, he felt too sad to leave his room.

Wednesday

I explore my library like someone returning to his native land after an absence of decades. Every time I leave on one of my book junkets, I have to chart its geography all over again, establish paths from shelf to shelf, remembering titles I have not thought about for weeks.

Like a man finding his bearings in a library, Holmes can trace his way through the labyrinth of London by reciting the names of the streets seen from a cab: "Wandsworth Road . . . Priory Road. Larkhall Lane. Stockwell Place. Robert Street. Coldharbour Lane." And later, the districts through which he pursues his quarry: "Streatham, Brixton, Camberwell . . . Kennington Lane . . . The Oval . . . Bond Street and Miles Street . . . Knight's Place." A city reduced to the titles it contains.

Imaginary libraries:

- A library of books never written: Sherlock Holmes's "small works," such as "a curious little work upon the influence of a trade upon the form of the hand, with lithotypes of the hands of slaters, sailors, cork-cutters, compositors, weavers, and diamond polishers," his monograph on the tracing of footsteps, and the celebrated *Upon the Distinction Between the Ashes of Various Tobaccos*, illustrated with colored plates.

- A library of real books read by imaginary characters: Holmes reads the German classics and, in order to support a Romantic view of the smallness of man in the universe, refers Watson to Jean Paul. Even more surprisingly, Watson replies that he has read him: "I worked back to him through Carlyle" (which elicits Holmes's comment "That was like following the brook to the parent lake").

Thursday

Holmes is a devotee of the now forgotten Winwood Reade, African explorer and unsuccessful roman-à-clef novelist whose *Martyrdom of Man* Holmes so enthusiastically recommends to Watson as "one of the most remarkable ever penned." Its bleak conclusion states, "But a season of mental anguish is at hand, and through this we must pass in order that our posterity may rise. The soul must be sacrificed; the hope in immortality must die." Like Winwood Reade, and in spite of the apparent duplicities in his creations—Holmes and Watson, Holmes and Moriarty—Conan Doyle seems to have believed in an integral unified world. (In one of his science fiction stories, "When the World Screamed," Professor Challenger proves that the planet is a single living animal by thrusting a gigantic needle deep into the earth, forcing it to scream.)

Sunday

Our neighbor, Mme M., tells us that the ghost of a certain mademoiselle haunts the place de la Mairie, but that, regrettably, she has never seen her.

Holmes (unlike his creator) doesn't believe in ghosts. Perhaps Conan Doyle's faith in the supernatural doesn't intrude in the world of Holmes because (in Conan Doyle's mind) it did not need to show itself in order to prove its existence. Solid flesh and ghostly presence, paladin and criminal, good man and evil were for Conan Doyle part of the same indistinguishable mesh, so that (in spite of Watson's scandalized bleatings) Holmes can burgle a safe or counterfeit a note, impersonate someone or lie to obtain the information he needs, and remain in the reader's view wholly trustworthy and heroic. These acts are more transgressions of manners than of morals, and Holmes is willing (the reader accepts this) to break the social code.

De Quincey: "For if once a man indulges himself in murder, very soon he comes to think little of robbing: and from robbing he comes next to drinking and Sabbath-breaking, and from that to incivility and procrastination."

Artificiality is of the essence. The vision of empire given through a clichéd description of the city—genteel London, London of the docks, London of the wicked foreigners—lends a fairy-tale quality to the Holmes saga. London or Baghdad, Holmes's city (that London I looked for when I first came to England and of course never found) is perfectly fictional, the reflection of an unreal reality. It is the London over which Peter Pan flies off to Never-Neverland, the London through which Dr. Jekyll seeks Mr. Hyde, the red-brick maze of Chesterton's nightmares, the decadent London of Beardsley and Wilde.

Thaddeus Sholto's Wildean apartment: "The richest and glossiest of curtains and tapestries draped the walls, looped back here and there to expose some richly mounted painting or Oriental vase. The carpet was of amber and black, so soft and so thick that the foot sank pleasantly into it, as into a bed of moss. Two great tiger-skins thrown athwart it increased the suggestion of Eastern luxury, as did a huge hookah which stood upon a mat in the corner. A lamp in the fashion of a silver dove was hung from an almost invisible golden wire in the centre of the room. As it burned it filled the air with a subtle and aromatic odour."

In the October evening light, my garden looks outrageously artificial.

Monday

Dickens's Mr. Podsnap in *Our Mutual Friend* rules Conan Doyle's class-conscious world. What is unfamiliar is evil, and must be rejected because it isn't English. It amuses me to read, in Naipaul's *Enigma of Arrival*, how he wants us to believe that a West Indian living in southern England in the 1950s would not be the butt of racial prejudice. I remember meeting for the first time my daughter's headmaster at her school in Kent, in the early nineties, and being greeted with a condescending "So you're the foreigner!"

Holmes picks up the poisoned dart that has killed Thaddeus Sholto's brother and hands it to Watson. "Is that an English thorn?" asks Holmes. "No," answers Watson (and the reader can hear his indignation at the suggestion), "it certainly is not."

Watson's own character was defined around 1650: "The true Heroick English Gentleman hath no Peer," Sir Thomas Browne wrote in *Christian Morals*.

Note: According to Sir George Sitwell, "the first English gentleman" was a certain Robert Erdeswick of Stafford, who in 1413 had to declare his social position at a trial in which he was accused of "housebreaking, wounding and incitement to murder."

Tuesday

The world seen from the vantage point of London: "The Hindu proper has long and thin feet," says Holmes. "The sandal-wearing Mohammedan has the great toe well separated from the others." Then he describes the inhabitants of the Andaman Islands, according to "the very latest authority" of a recently published gazetteer: "They are a fierce, morose, and intractable people, though capable of forming most devoted friendships when their confidence has once been gained . . . They are naturally hideous, having large, misshapen heads, small, fierce eyes, and distorted features. Their feet and hands, however, are remarkably small. So intractable and fierce are they that all the efforts of the British officials have failed to win them over in any degree."

Marco Denevi: "Recently expelled from paradise, Adam made a spectacular appearance among the animals. They all immediately recognized in him someone stronger than any creature in the sea or the sky or on earth. But while some, to free themselves of the obligation to seek their own sustenance, ran up to bow before him, others, proud of their freedom and their individuality, preferred to keep themselves apart. These latter ones Adam called *the wild beasts.*"

Point of view: when Watson is reflecting on the mysterious murder and looks back at Miss Morstan's house, it isn't only the thought of the woman he loves that consoles him. "It was soothing," he writes, "to catch even that passing glimpse of a tranquil English home in the midst of the wild, dark business which had absorbed us." The adjectives are significant.

Wednesday

I'm astonished by the ease with which British xenophobia of the late nineteenth century slips into a particularly nasty anti-Semitism in the twentieth. By the ease with which the Jewish caricature is introduced into the plot of the detective novels of the golden age: Agatha Christie, John Dickson Carr, Dorothy L. Sayers, E. C. R. Lorac . . . Even before Hitler, there seems to be, in the British imagination, a fixed caricature of the Jew, often damned with ludicrous praise, as in Anthony Berkeley's *The Silk Stocking Murders*. The detective is an English gentleman, Roger Sheringham; his assistant, the murdered woman's sister, Anne; the murderer (revealed in the last pages, of course) is a suave, rich, refined Jew called Pleydell. After meeting him, Anne comments, "I've never met a Jew I liked so much before."

"The real pure blooded Jew," Roger tells her, "is one of the best fellows in the world. It's the hybrid Jew, the Russian and Polish and German variety, that's let the race down so badly."

This is England, in 1941, a year after the creation of Auschwitz.

Friday

The wind last night broke a branch of one of the sophora trees, the one that is practically hollow. Nothing serious. C. wonders how a hollow tree can keep on living, sprouting new leaves every year.

I return to this notion of balance. The foreigner (like the criminal) destroys the agreed-upon equilibrium. The world must be restored to a clear-cut vocabulary of white and black. There can be no ambiguity in the detective novel, at least not in the "classic" detective novel. Browning's lines,

> Our interest's on the dangerous edge of things.
> The honest thief, the tender murderer,
> The superstitious atheist, demi-rep
> That loves and saves her soul in new French books . . .

cannot apply to the Holmes saga.

Graham Greene said that the Browning quotation could stand as an epigraph to any of his books. In *The Power and the Glory* he wrote, "When you visualized a man or a woman carefully, you could always begin to feel pity . . . That was a quality God's image carried with it . . . when you saw the lines at the corners of the eyes, the shape of the mouth, how the hair grew, it was impossible to hate. Hate was just a failure of the imagination."

Kierkegaard: "Most people really believe that the Christian commandments (e.g., to love one's neighbour as oneself) are intentionally a little too severe—like putting the clock ahead half an hour to make sure of not being late in the morning."

Saturday

Thick, heavy rain. Impossible to see halfway down the garden. I have to imagine what is there: the back wall with the fig tree and the vines, the small cherry orchard (can an orchard contain only four trees?), the large drooping pines, the quartet of white birches where the hedgehogs like to hide.

Doyle quotes Goethe again at the end of the book (the lines are from *Xenian*, which Goethe wrote with Schiller in 1796): *"Schade dass die Natur nur einen Mensch aus dir schuf, / Denn zum würdigen Mann war und zum Schelmen der Stroff."* ("Unfortunately Nature made only one man out of you, / Although there was material for both a good man and a scoundrel.")

A variation on the theme of the double: the sleuth as criminal. Numerous detective novels (since Israel Zangwill's *The Big Bow Mystery* of 1892) play on this conceit. Perfectly appropriate to describe the balance in Holmes's double nature (perhaps not far from Wilde's Dorian Gray), these words spoken by Watson: "So swift, silent, and furtive were his movements, like those of a trained bloodhound picking out a scent, that I could not but think what a terrible criminal he would have made had he turned his energy and sagacity against the law instead of exerting them in its defence."

Sunday

Watson marries Miss Morstan. He tells Holmes, "Miss Morstan has done me the honour to accept me as a husband in the prospective."

(To which Holmes the inveterate bachelor replies, "I really cannot congratulate you.") Watson's romance has always made me uncomfortable—as a child, because I squirmed when I had to witness adult displays of sexual affection; now, because I find the relationship so utterly unbelievable. Maybe that is the reason for the learned confusion regarding Watson's wedded life in the Conan Doyle canon (whether Watson married Miss Morstan secretly before the events narrated in *The Sign of Four*, whether she died in "The Adventure of the Empty House," whether Watson married again in "The Adventure of the Blanched Soldier" and, if he did, who the second Mrs. Watson was).

Monday

The rain has stopped. For several weeks now I've followed a certain routine: working on one book in the morning, on another in the afternoon. This is easier now that the days are getting colder. Two different voices or tones: the first tries to be coherent and follows the thread of a narrative or an argument; the second (this diary) is fragmented, haphazard. The second allows me to think without an established destination.

The reader contradicts the writer's method, whatever that may be. As a reader, I'll follow a carefully plotted story carelessly, allowing myself to be distracted by details and aleatory thoughts; on the other hand, I'll read a fragmentary work (Valéry, for instance, or Pío Baroja) as if I were connecting the dots, in search of order. In both cases, however, I look for (or imagine) a link between beginning and end, as if all reading were, in its very nature, circular. Maybe Joyce intuited this quality of reading when he decided to lock in the chaos of *Finnegans Wake. The Sign of Four* ends as it begins: with Holmes reaching for the cocaine bottle.

On the door to my library I've written a variation on the motto of Rabelais' Abbey of Thelême: LYS CE QUE VOUDRA ("Read what you will").

NOVEMBER

Monday

Back in Canada.

I'm in Calgary for a short visit, to attend a conference at the Banff Centre for the Arts. The city seems to have extended itself in the past few years, allotment after identical allotment, an unstoppable growth, a horrible imitation of the American Midwestern model made up of crowded monstrosities with no urban heart—no squares, no schools, no churches, no small shops. What kind of dialogue or communication can take place in communities like these?

When I first read Goethe's *Elective Affinities*—twenty-five years ago at least—I did so after a long conversation with Hector Bianciotti on Marivaux's *La dispute*, which he had seen in Lavelli's production and which I had had to miss because I couldn't afford the price of the ticket. Like so many other Marivaux plays, *La dispute* explores the nature of love: two aristocratic characters wish to resolve the question of who is more likely to be unfaithful, man or woman, and in order to reach an answer they place four children in solitary seclusion, each looked after by a couple of "savages." Only once the children reach the age of puberty are they allowed to meet, and the aristocrats, from a scientific distance, can then observe and study their behavior.

Hector loved above all the final moment in Lavelli's production, when, the experiment concluded, the aristocrats are about to cross over onto the island where the children are kept, but stop at the edge of the bridge; at this point the curtain falls. For Hector, the aristocrats' true character lay in this hesitation: to observe but not to experience. (Earlier he had noticed the same hesitation in the film version of Hartley's *The Go-Between*, when the matriarch refuses to go and see for herself her daughter's infidelity.)

Somewhere I read that King Frederick II tried to conduct a similar experiment, not on the nature of love but on the nature of language. In order to discover what our "original" language was, he ordered that a number of newborn babes be tended by wet nurses who were forbidden to speak to them; in this way he imagined he might hear the first words spoken "naturally," untaught. The experiment failed because none of the babies lived. Apparently we need language as we need food, in order to survive.

That an experiment is doomed to failure doesn't make it, of course, ineffective. In *Werther*, Goethe facetiously remarks, "If mutual trust had earlier brought them together again, if love and understanding had helped them open their hearts to each other, our friend might still have been saved." Not so, as *Elective Affinities* proves, because it is in the characters' own nature that they must fail, and in that failure lies the novel's success.

Tuesday

Elective Affinities has something of a soap-opera plot centered around its four main characters: the middle-aged Eduard and Charlotte, who loved each other in their youth, drifted apart and then finally married after their partners died; and Ottilie and the Captain, their long-term guests, with whom they fall respectively in love.

"Fate," says Charlotte, late in the book, "takes command of certain matters, and is very stubborn. Reason and virtue, duty and everything sacred oppose it in vain; things are likely to happen that seem justified to Fate but not to us; and so Fate asserts itself, whatever choices we make." And then she realizes the truth, which sounds like an accusation: "But what am I saying! In fact, Fate is trying to carry out my own wishes and intentions, which I, in my thoughtlessness, have acted against."

I am puzzled and enchanted by this realization. Charlotte argues that Fate knows *better* than herself her own intentions. What is this Fate that is wiser than the protagonists? Not the Fate (in the guise of Death) of Cocteau's story in *Le grand écart*, as helpless as his victims to know the future:

> A young gardener said to his prince, "Save me! I met Death in the garden this morning and he made a menacing gesture. Tonight I wish by some miracle I could be far away, in Ispahan."
>
> The prince lent him his swiftest horse.
>
> That afternoon, walking in the garden, the prince came face to face with Death. "Why," he asked, "did you make a threatening gesture at my gardener this morning?"

> "It wasn't a threatening gesture," answered Death. "It was a gesture of surprise. I saw him far from Ispahan this morning, and I knew that I must take him in Ispahan tonight."

Eduard and Charlotte, the aristocratic gardeners in *Elective Affinities*, never shy away from the encounters that Fate prepares for them (even if sometimes they arrive, as Charlotte does, a little late). They merely follow the plot: Fate as story.

Where does this notion come from? I wonder. Not from the *imaginaire* of the Greeks, as Paul Veyne makes clear in his lovingly written book on the "constitutive imagination," as he calls it, *Did the Greeks Believe in Their Myths?* The notion belongs to literature, or rather to the reading of literature, when the reader accepts what he reads as fiction and yet "willingly suspends disbelief" for the sake of the story; this is what we mean by the inevitability of the plot. All business is conducted between the characters and the reader; the author is absent, or (in the case of Goethe) he is merely a master of ceremonies who comments on but has no say in his characters' behaviour.

The youthful Stephen Dedalus has this to say in Joyce's *Portrait of the Artist as a Young Man*:

> The personality of the artist, at first a cry or a cadence or a mood and then a fluid and lambent narrative, finally refines itself out of existence, impersonalises itself, so to speak . . . The artist, like the God of creation, remains within or behind or beyond or above his handiwork, invisible, refined out of existence, indifferent, paring his fingernails.

Today, playing with hypertext in the postmodernist sandbox, where we have the illusion of diverting the plot down a finite number of paths, we are like Eduard and Charlotte and Ottilie and the Captain; we choose possibilities that Fate (like an authoritative parent) has already chosen for us.

I'm reminded of Nathaniel Hawthorne, who jotted down this idea for a story in one of his astounding notebooks:

> A person to be writing a tale, and to find that it shapes itself against his intentions: that the characters act otherwise than he thought: that unforeseen events occur; and a catastrophe comes which he strives in vain to avert. It might shadow forth his own fate—he having made himself one of the personages.

Wednesday

The Palliser Hotel in Calgary looks incongruously European in this Midwestern setting, like something out of Henry James. I sit in a red velvet armchair among potted palms, waiting for the car to take me to Banff, and watch the characters enter and exit a story.

Goethe never bothers with architecture in his novels. And though I wrote that he has no say in his characters' behaviour, this formality isn't coldness; one senses a raging passion behind the gilded façade, something torn between emotion, duty and an ultimate sense of helplessness. When Eduard, Charlotte and the Captain are discussing the elective affinities in chemistry and comparing them to human relationships, one knows that the carefully arranged words, exchanged as in one of those philosophical dialogues dear to Hobbes and Newton, betray a turmoil that is kept unseen, a rawness that (I like to think) is Goethe's own. My fondness for the old man comes, I believe, from that brittle combination of strength and delicacy. There are times when the clean and proper shell of his prose moves me to tears, for the sake of the darkness it covers.

Like his beloved Diderot, Goethe always seems to be laying his working tools out for the reader's inspection. There is a startling self-assurance in this, like a magician inviting the public to inspect his bag of tricks. Eduard, criticizing the author of the book he's reading, calls the man "a true Narcissus: he finds his own image everywhere and sees the entire world against the background of his own self." This *Bespiegelung* or "mirroring" is, of course, Goethe's own, or rather, that of his characters.

The Colombian Fernando Vallejo, explaining why he will not second-guess his characters' thoughts: "I am a *first-person* novelist."

The physical landscape of Goethe's novel becomes the landscape of the characters' emotions; they attempt to domesticate nature much as they attempt to plan their affinities on an actual chart. Nature is seen as a sort of *carte de Tendre*, the seventeenth-century allegorical map that traces the way to the loved one's heart. Charlotte's garden, for instance, is too easy a symbol for their experiment in the human world (the hut that can fit two, or three or, as Charlotte heavily adds, "even a fourth," etc.), and yet it matches the artificial tone of their dialogue—artificial, at least, to my foreign ears. There is something of the maxim-collector in their speeches (Charlotte ending the chapter with "And yet in many cases . . . it is kinder and more useful to write nothing of import, than not to write at all"). How different the tone, a little later in the book, when the irreversible nature of the present is described, and another voice, intuition or experience, not the mere imitation of Lichtenberg's aphorisms or the Book of Proverbs, calls out, "And yet the present will not be deprived of its terrible rights. They spent part of the night in amusing conversation, which seemed all the freer because the heart unfortunately had no part in it." These words are spoken from an intimate, visceral understanding of such a moment, one we all recognize.

Laurence Olivier was once asked how he managed to utter Oedipus's now famous piercing cry of pain. "I heard about how they catch ermine," he explained. "In the Arctic, they put down salt and the ermine comes to lick it. And his tongue freezes to the ice. I thought about that when I screamed in Oedipus." An absolute grasp of a moment of truth.

"These analogies," says Charlotte, "are effective and entertaining, and who would not gladly amuse himself with such similarities?"

Thursday

This morning, I read in the Calgary paper that once again the provincial government intends to cut all manner of social programs, including support for handicapped people. A legally blind man, whose wife was suffering from multiple sclerosis and couldn't work, was threatened with having his government payments cut off because he had taken a part-time job. His disability benefit amounted to $800 Canadian a month; no one can live on that amount, paying for rent and food. The statistics of child poverty in Alberta are astounding, especially in one of the richest provinces in one of the richest countries on earth. In 1996, for instance, the number of children living below the poverty line was 148,000.

What did I do about any of this?

I feel like Mittler, the fifth character in *Elective Affinities*, the outsider who, on the one hand, will not "waste his time in any household where there was no help to give and no quarrel to resolve," and on the other, haughtily refuses to help out his best friends. Even though he fails, he seems to me to be a worthy *Mittler* (the word means "mediator"). "Those who are superstitious about names," we are told, "maintain that the name Mittler had obligated him to take on this strangest of all vocations." If so, my name would echo perhaps my countless *Mangeln* ("faults" in German), if *Mangelhaftigkeit* ("inadequacy") is my lot. The English etymology is kinder, associating my name with "among" or "a person among many"—in other words, one of Dr. Johnson's "common readers."

Saturday

Back home to France. Every time I return, I'm astonished to see, after the immense Prairie skies, the stinginess of the skies in European cities.

Goethe seems to be always thinking; anywhere you go in his writing, there is never pure narration, there's always conscious, articulated thought, permeating every room like the smell of fried onions. I enjoy this pervasiveness; a character can't make a simple gesture without its being reflected upon, after being caught in the all-seeing eye of this minor god. The omniscient Goethe; this reminds me of a calligraphic sign that hung in the bedroom of a schoolmate of mine when we were both nine or ten, in Buenos Aires:

> Remember that God is watching you,
> Remember He's watching; then,
> Remember that you are going to die,
> And remember, you don't know when.

Both observer and observed are present in the brief scene (and intellectual reflection) in which Eduard, reading out loud, crankily complains of Charlotte reading over his shoulder. "If I read to someone, isn't it just the same as if I were explaining something orally? The written or printed words take the place of my own feelings and intentions, and do you think I would take the trouble to talk intelligibly if there were a window in my forehead or my breast, so that the person to whom I wish to relate my thoughts and feelings one by one knew in advance what I was aiming at? When someone reads over my shoulder, I always feel as if I were split in two."

Here speaks a true reader, aware of the protocols of reading and jealous of his reading space, which must be one of three: either entirely private, silent and collected; or shared, silent as well, like the reading of Dante's Paolo and Francesca, whose eyes and then lips meet across a page; or shared through reading out loud, when the possession of the page is that of the reader exclusively, never that of the listener. The duplicity that Eduard feels—"split in two"—is that of simultaneous modes of reading that contradict each other. Ottilie writes in her diary, "Each word that is spoken gives rise to its opposite."

Also, the question here is that of the performance of fiction. The narrative act must exist in the time allotted for its telling, and the reader-accomplice (in this case the listener-accomplice) must not jump forward to the text's conclusion, since this would shorten, as it were, the life of the story. (That conclusion is the forbidden last page of the magic book in fairy tales . . .)

Midnight

In Turkish, the word *muhabbet* means both "conversation" and "love." You say for both, "To do *muhabbet.*" I like the idea of conversation being a window into one's heart or mind.

Sunday

I've looked at two translations of *Elective Affinities* in English: one by David Carradine, published by Oxford University Press; the other by Judith Ryan, published by Princeton. Neither is fully satisfying, but both, as the French say, *se laissent lire*. Goethe suggested, in one of his many letters to Wilhelm von Humboldt, that national languages reflect the national character, and that English writers share with the Germans the same ways of thinking and the same sense of what is precious. This would explain why Shakespeare is part of the German tradition; it does not explain why

Goethe never became part of the English tradition. Somehow, "Gouty" (to use Joyce's disrespectful epithet) hasn't lodged in the English-reading canon in his successive incarnations. Even though the first full-length biography of Goethe in *any* language was written by the multitalented George Henry Lewes in 1855, and in spite of Goethe's influence on writers such as Lewes's partner, George Eliot (I remember the *Elective Affinities*–like ending of *The Mill on the Floss*), he has few English readers.

In Buenos Aires, when I was growing up in the late fifties and early sixties, many of my friends came from German Jewish families. Goethe and Schiller were conventional staples of the ancient, all-embracing German *Kultur* that the immigrants had brought in their cardboard suitcases and knotted bundles. In Germany, Schiller (and Goethe) had long lost their dreadful local accents; in the Diaspora, Goethe (and Schiller) had acquired the tone and humor of the shtetl. Whenever a discussion broke out among the German parents of my friends, the one about to lose the argument would shout, *"'O aza nar,' sagt Goethe"* ("'Oh, what a fool!,' says Goethe"), to which the other would counter, *"'Nebisch,' sagt Schiller"* ("'You nitwit,' says Schiller"), and the battle would end with a comforting laugh.

Perhaps the void in the English-speaking world exists because Goethe must be entered culturally: not book by book, dipping one's toe in his writings, but rather by plunging into his vast influence, his oceanic scope, his echoing waves, his horizon-reaching vistas of the world. "I'll goethe you lot," our teacher told us on the first day of class at the Pestalozzi Schule (the German school in Buenos Aires, which I attended for a single year), and made us learn by heart "Erlkönig" and *"Es war ein König in Thule"* and "Ginkgo Biloba."

Nietzsche, seldom generous in his praise, saw Goethe as uniquely above nationalities and national literatures. "Goethe," he wrote in *Human, All Too Human*, "is not just a good and great human being but a civilization in himself." If that is so, then *Elective Affinities*, written in the last years of his life, reads like a kind of etiquette manual of Goethean civilization.

Note: Goethe wanted to give his son August a toy guillotine for his twelfth birthday. August's mother, Christiane, was indignant.

Evening

The mock-mathematical formulations to outline human behaviour that Goethe puts in Eduard's mouth ("Look out, my friend, for D! What will B do when C is taken away from him? . . . He'll go back to his A, his alpha and omega!") echo in the tests published in our lifestyle magazines. Are you a good lover? Are you a dutiful citizen? Are you a happy person? Tick the boxes and find the formula that applies to you. These are forms of consolation, I suppose, to allow for the illusion that we're not living in ambiguity.

Monday

Charlotte, the architect who supervised the building of our library, tells us that she is planning the new public swimming pool in a nearby village. It needs to be practical, of course, large enough to house the crowds expected every summer, but also emblematic of the mayor's ambitions, something "grand and modern" as well as "neat and clean." I suggest that all architecture is unavoidably symbolic. "Unfortunately," she says.

I've reached the moment in the novel when Eduard and the Captain are dabbling in urbanism, discussing the creation of a village that will follow not the Swiss style of architecture but merely the Swiss style "of neatness and cleanliness." A beggar comes up to them, asking for alms. Eduard, upset at being interrupted, angrily dismisses him. The man withdraws "with small steps," defending "the right of beggars," "who could be refused alms but should not be insulted because they were as much under the protection of God and the king as anyone else."

The Captain's solution to the problem of begging—systematizing the almsgiving by depositing a sum with an elderly couple who would pay beggars at the exit (not the entrance) of the village—once again resonates for me when I think of the cities I've lived in: Calgary, Toronto, Buenos Aires, Paris, London. It is, like the mathematical formula devised to explain away emotions, a method for *not* recognizing the humanity of those in need. I must remember: this is not Goethe; this is the Captain speaking.

Once, as I sat reading on the Paris Métro, a beggar reciting the usual litany of "*Mesdames et messieurs*, I apologize for disturbing you, etc., etc." from coach to coach suddenly threw down the newspapers that justified his begging and shouted at us, "Look at me! All I want you to do is look at me! I'm a human being too, for goodness' sake! Look at me, you bastards, under your winter coats you're all like me!"

Eduard and Charlotte, Ottilie and the Captain feel that their ideas about love place them outside the common circle of society, just as we, the readers, bound by our own convictions, feel outside the reality of fiction, unwilling even to imagine that we, too, are the Red King's dream.

In Lenz's *Der Waldbruder*, his companion piece to *Werther*, the character based on Goethe writes, "All this contrasts so dreadfully with our style of love."

Tuesday

The postwoman brings the daily gossip: someone leaving, someone dead, someone getting married. The house at the corner of the village will be rented to a nurse from the local hospital.

Goethe: "Everything seemed to take its accustomed course. For even in the most terrible situations, when everything is at stake, people live on as if it were nothing of importance." That meekness is always surprising. Auden, in his poem on Brueghel's painting of Icarus falling into the sea, observed that the Old Masters were never wrong about suffering, "how it takes place / While someone else is eating or opening a window or just walking dully along." I think of how life went on in Argentina during the military dictatorship, people continuing with their daily lives while their neighbors were being kidnapped and tortured, or pushed into a plane and dropped manacled into the river—continuing with their shopping, their social calls, their worries about prices and the weather—as news drifted through from time to time about a mysterious disappearance or a late-night arrest, together with excuses half believed in, that maybe the neighbors were on holidays, maybe they'd been involved in some criminal activities, maybe they'd moved, and everything seemingly normal, their daily routine uninterrupted, even though, as Auden says, they "must have seen / Something amazing, a boy falling out of the sky, / Had somewhere to get to and sailed calmly on."

Goethe has this to say about Eduard's love for Ottilie: "Secretly, he had given himself over completely to the feeling of his passion." This is, in some sense, the emotional equivalent of that political passivity—self-absorption masquerading as passion.

Friday

I could compose a diary made exclusively of fragments from other diaries. This would reflect my habit of thinking in quotations.

Saturday

From Ottilie's diary:

- "Life without love, without the physical presence of the one you love, is nothing but a '*comédie à tiroir*,' a conventional farce." And later: "Politeness of heart": an extraordinary concept, and so true, immediately recognizable. It is what Chateaubriand calls the emotion in which love is no longer a rapture and has not yet become a "passionate friendship."
- "No one wanders under palm trees unpunished, and the way one behaves no doubt must change in a place where

elephants and tigers make their home." Or the contrary, of course. This much-quoted line of Ottilie's is for me, the wanderer, deeply ironic, since it was under palm trees (when I was working for a publishing company in Tahiti during the seventies) that I decided to be true to myself and accept my life as a reader-writer. Every sojourn "under palm trees" is an exile. Ovid weeps at being in a foreign land; Cortázar rejoices in having left Argentina for Paris. And in both cases the imagination is fed by novelty or by contrast.

- "One always imagines oneself seeing. I think we dream merely to prevent ourselves from ceasing to see." This precise description of human consciousness, of its terrible, Argus-like wakefulness, gives the whole novel its pathos: the four characters, the author and by extension the reader are constantly aware of their actions, and watch themselves hurtle toward their end without being able to deceive themselves or look away.

Monday

The books that pile up by the side of my bed appear to read themselves out loud to me in my sleep. Before turning off the light, I leaf through one of them, I read a couple of paragraphs, put it aside, take up another. After a few days, I have the impression of knowing them all.

Among the books by my bed tonight:

- Wayne Johnston, *The Colony of Unrequited Dreams*

- Enrique Vila-Matas, *Bartleby y compañía*
- Ellery Queen, *The Vanishing Corpse*
- Ian McEwan, *Enduring Love*
- Stefan George, *Der siebente Ring*
- W. G. Sebald, *Luftkrieg und Literatur*
- Ryu Murakami, *Almost Transparent Blue*
- Dorothy L. Sayers and Jill Paton Walsh, *Thrones, Dominations*
- Jacques Le Goff, *La naissance du Purgatoire*
- Max Rouquette, *Ils sont les bergers des étoiles*

Each of these books capriciously influences my reading of the one next to it. Is all reading associative reading?

I go through the final pages of *Elective Affinities* once again. The last time I read them I was in Calgary, and I remember snow falling very persistently on the street and the tree outside, filling in any spaces of color, covering any faults. Goethe had been there too, of course. In one of his collections of maxims he wrote, "Snow is a fictitious cleanliness." Indeed.

When I lived in Calgary, the papers reported that a native man had been found frozen to death on a bench downtown; the alcohol in his blood had increased the hypothermia, and he lay there, the snow not falling fast enough to hide him from public view. We are each supposed to do our thing, play our role. And what role would that be?

Thursday

C., accustomed to the rules of Canadian weather, is surprised by the fact that he can plant flowers in our garden as late as November. He has just planted cuttings of Maria Callas roses, a gift from our neighbor. The plot, with its handwritten sign, looks like a little graveyard in which the singer lies buried. From a poem by Stefan George: *Nun lerne Trauer/und Ernst von Rosen*. ("Now learn sadness / and seriousness from the roses.")

Is that what *Elective Affinities* is anachronistically parodying? Can it be read as a cynical apotheosis of the art of gardening, the art that flourished in the eighteenth century and became a subverted ecology—what one might call a supremacist view of nature, even—reflected, almost a century and a half later, in Hitler's concern with "the model of nature"? "We must leave room for pastures," Hitler explained to Martin Bormann over dinner, on September 28, 1941. "Nature has made the various regions of the earth in such a way as to ensure a sort of autarky for each." Earth, for the players in the game of elective affinities, is a frame for their own ambitions: they are each like a little Adam entrusted with the run of Eden, and they can judge each region of the earth accordingly and yet be themselves blind to their Author's judgment. Planting their roses, redesigning their gardens and tending their trees, they neglect their own lives.

Saturday

The conclusion of *Elective Affinities*, for me, lies not on the book's last page but on the deathbed of Joseph Roth, in Paris, on May 22,

1939. Exhausted and bewildered, Roth hears whispered stories about the crimes at Buchenwald and an image comes to him: there, in what was once called Ettersberg, stands Goethe's oak, under whose generous shadow the Master used to meet his beloved Frau von Stein. Now, casting that same shadow over the laundry and kitchen of the newly built concentration camp, the oak continues to stand, safeguarded by the so-called Nature Protection Act of the Third Reich. And Roth, with his last breath, utters his comment, beyond rage and beyond irony:

> Every day, the inmates of the concentration camp walk by and around the oak tree; that is to say, they are made to walk by there. Indeed! Misinformation is being spread about the Buchenwald Concentration Camp—horror stories, one might say. It seems to me the time has come to put things in the right perspective. Until now, not a single inmate of the concentration camp has been strapped to the oak tree under which Goethe and Frau von Stein sat, which is still alive, thanks to the "Nature Protection Act." Certainly not; they have been strapped to other oaks, of which there is no shortage in this forest *{an denen es in diesem Wald nicht mangelt}*.

(I suddenly realize that, due to a fortuitous etymology, I, one future reader among countless readers, am included in the very last word he wrote.)

With this vision, this joke, this heart-shattering observation, Joseph Roth dies.

DECEMBER

Sunday

The house, which we bought two years ago, is a wonderful house, a magical house. It rises on a small hill where once stood a temple to Dionysus, now replaced by a church dedicated to Saint Martin. The church, with which we share a wall, dates back to the thirteenth century, so we believe that the house was built around that time, and then was enlarged four or five centuries later. The adjacent barn collapsed in the early 1800s; last spring we had the walls restored and it now holds the library. Together, both buildings form an open square, each truncated end marked by a pigeon tower. Beyond lies the garden, and a small orchard planted over what was once the cemetery, so that the plums, cherries, figs and nuts that we are promised in the summer have fed on ancient bones. After we first saw the house, in the fall of 2000, I dreamt constantly of it, perhaps because I hadn't owned a place, a home to call mine, for the past ten years. We had rented here and there and made believe the places we lived in were ours, but now this house, unbelievably, is home.

Two Decembers ago, I sat in the Grand Hotel in Poitiers, waiting for the owners of the house to agree on a date for the signing, and read *The Wind in the Willows*. I've picked it up again, to celebrate our second Christmas in the house. I don't remember when I read it first, or what I thought of it then, but I've always felt a fondness for it, without knowing precisely why. Reading it now, I realize that my choice was exactly right. *The Wind in the Willows* is all about home. In the midst of something like despair (would we ever find the right place?) and nostalgia (remember the view from the kitchen window of the small house in Toronto? remember the fireplace? the tin mouldings on the ceiling?) I come across this line: "We're going to find that home of yours, old fellow" (this is Rat speaking), "so you had better come along, for it will take some finding, and we shall want your nose."

Nose, of course, is what we always need.

Monday

There is something like snow in the air, but not quite, just enough to remind us of December in Canada. We miss the snow. Rat: "Snow makes everything look so very different."

We sit in the kitchen, under the stained beams. The main one was replaced soon after we moved in, more than a year ago, a memorable operation. It was rotten, held up by a wooden column that looked like a gallows, and so soft that we could stick a knife into it as if it were butter. A new beam was needed, and the carpenter discovered one in a nearby village. It's five meters long and almost two centuries old; five men were required to carry it.

There is an image in the back of my mind (an engraving?) of people transporting the skeleton of a whale from Portsmouth to London.

Wednesday

According to Alan Bennett, *The Wind in the Willows* is Mole's bildungsroman. Mole is content as long as he isn't adventurous. Contentment requires a certain lack of curiosity.

I remember that, shortly after I left Buenos Aires in 1968, I became convinced that I would never live in the same place for more than two years at a time. So I spent periods of two years in Barcelona, Paris, London, Milan, Tahiti . . . Then I settled in Canada and everything changed. Now I'm suddenly flooded by the certainty of places I won't live in, things I won't do, roles I won't play: a huge cosmic pageant that excludes me completely.

Unutterable relief.

Afternoon

I like Mr. Badger very much. He doesn't mind a certain neglect of manners, "nor did he take any notice of elbows on the table, or everybody speaking at once. As he did not go into Society himself, he had got an idea that these things belonged to the things that didn't really matter."

Note: It might be useful to compile a list of "things that don't really matter." Such a list would enormously alleviate my daily lot of worrying.

Toad, on the other hand, I don't like. He is exactly like a certain kind of schoolmate who always used to appear, under different names and guises, in all my classes, annoying because a braggart and pitiful because a coward. And a snob, too. Mavis remembers being horrified by Toad's attack on the barge-woman he meets during his ignominious escape. "You common, low, *fat* barge-woman!" he shouted; "don't you dare to talk to your betters like that! . . . I would have you know that I am a Toad, a very well-known respected, distinguished Toad! I may be under a bit of a cloud at present, but I will *not* be laughed at by a barge-woman!"

Friday

Very cold but sunny. For a few hours this morning every leaf of grass, every twig was covered with brilliant furlike frost. The garden looks uncanny.

When Rat and Mole, lost in the snowstorm in the Wild Wood, finally knock on Mr. Badger's door, they hear "the sound of slow shuffling footsteps approaching the door from the inside," which seems to Mole "like some one walking in carpet slippers that were too large for him and down-at-heel." That shuffling sound reminds me of the terrifying moment in Kipling's story "The Wish House" when the unseen creature that is able to grant wishes moves behind the closed door like "a heavy woman in slippers." The sound that is comforting in *The Wind in the Willows* turns nightmarish in "The Wish House."

Monday

Richard Outram tells C. that Barbara, his wife, died last night. Her engravings, with Richard's poems, hang upstairs in the house.

C. has a fiery landscape by her—orange, yellow and purple—in his office; it illuminates the room. It seems impossible that we will never see her, speak with her, again. Ever.

I am furious at the taking away of things, at these brutal changes. And the older I get, the faster changes happen: friends disappear, landscapes clutter. I want my friends to be there always, I want the places I like to stay the same. I want there to be certain fixed points in the universe on which I can count. I don't want to keep missing voices, faces, names. I want to be able to move around blindfolded. I don't want to have to learn my way around a room again and again. I want to be able to start conversations without any kind of preamble or introduction.

There is a long passage in *The Wind in the Willows*, at the end of the chapter in which Mole finds his old house again, that I want to quote in its entirety:

> The weary Mole also was glad to turn in without delay, and soon had his head on his pillow, in great joy and contentment. But ere he closed his eyes he let them wander round his old room, mellow in the glow of the firelight that played or rested on familiar and friendly things which had long been unconsciously a part of him, and now smilingly received him back, without rancour . . . He saw clearly how plain and simple—how narrow, even—it all was; but clearly, too, how much it all meant to him, and the special value of some such anchorage in one's existence. He did not at all want to abandon the new life and its splendid spaces, to turn his back on sun and air and all they offered him and creep home and stay there; the upper world was all too strong, it called to him still, even down there, and he knew

he must return to the larger stage. But it was good to think he had this to come back to, this place which was all his own, these things which were so glad to see him again and could always be counted upon for the same simple welcome.

Midnight

The word "nostalgia" was invented on June 22, 1688, by Johannes Hofer, an Alsatian medical student, by combining the word *nostos* ("return") with the word *algos* ("pain") in his medical thesis, *Dissertatio medica de nostalgia*, to describe the sickness of Swiss soldiers kept far away from their mountains.

Friday

Kenneth Grahame is masterly at describing comfort: "The Badger's winter stores, which indeed were visible everywhere, took up half the room—piles of apples, turnips, and potatoes, baskets full of nuts, and jars of honey; but the two little white beds on the remainder of the floor looked soft and inviting, and the linen on them, though coarse, was clean and smelt beautifully of lavender." Reading a description like this, especially in my adolescence, made me fantasize for hours about a place of my own, and what it would look like.

Thirteen years before writing *The Wind in the Willows*, Grahame had a dream. He found himself in "a certain little room, very dear and familiar . . . solitary, the world walled out, but full of a brooding sense of peace and possession . . . All was modest—O, so very modest! But all was my very own, and what was more, everything in the room was exactly right."

A few times I have had the sense of "everything in the room" being "exactly right."

Later

I can tell what it will be like to live in a certain house as soon as I cross the threshold. The empathy (or lack of) is immediate. In the sixteenth-century picaresque novel *El Lazarillo de Tormes*, the hero notes, "There are unhappy and ill-rooted houses that stick their misfortune onto those who live in them." The same is true of places that are joyful.

This evening we start wrapping Christmas presents.

Sunday

Grahame wisely divides adventurers into those who like their adventures orderly and those who prefer the thrill of chaos. "Mole saw clearly that he was an animal of tilled field and hedgerow, linked to the ploughed furrow, the frequented pasture, the lane of evening lingerings, the cultivated garden-plot. For others the asperities, the stubborn endurance, or the clash of actual conflict, that went with Nature in the rough; he must be wise, must keep to the pleasant places in which his lines were laid and which held adventure enough, in their way, to last for a lifetime."

I think I am like Mole in this.

Explaining "home": in today's *New York Times*, the announcement that the Bush administration has recruited "prominent American writers" to explain the United States to Muslim countries. In spite of "congressional fears of the government propagandizing the American people," writers such as Richard Ford, Julia Alvarez, Robert Pinsky, Sven Birkerts, Robert Olen Butler and Bharati Mukherjee agreed to contribute to an all-American Festschrift. True, at all times great writers have lent their voices to political propaganda (Virgil's *Aeneid* was for Augustus a handy justification for his claim to divine power), and yet it still astonishes me to see with what naïveté writers as intelligent as Pinsky allow their work to be used by their government. Phrases such as "being an American, and a writer no less, has served me very well indeed" (Richard Ford) will do little to temper the loathing that American policies have bred in most countries around the world.

Chesterton on patriotism: "'My country right or wrong' . . . is like saying, 'My mother drunk or sober.'"

Monday

Ovid's *Tristia*, the poems he wrote after he had been exiled to the dreadful outpost of Tomis by Augustus, are mostly in the form of letters to friends and enemies, lamenting his absence from Rome and his loneliness in the barren, treeless landscape. *The Wind in the Willows* is the reverse of Ovid's *Tristia*.

I have never felt in exile, unlike so many of the writers I've met. I remember the Cuban group in Paris, clustered around the novelist Severo Sarduy, always conscious of not being in the place they had been compelled to leave. Sarduy was very aware that exile had made him nostalgic for a country that no longer existed, perhaps had never existed, at least as he remembered it—a country created by layers and layers of memory, embroidered, corrected, reshaped. He believed that even the places we live in become transformed through our prejudices, whims, limited experience, through the fact that we walk one route and not another from our house to the baker's, or that we choose one café, one park, one grocer from the variety of sites that make up a certain city. In this sense, every place is imaginary.

Sarduy used the description Columbus gave of Cuba (which the admiral believed was India) to describe a visit he himself made to India, nostalgic for Cuba.

For the exile, time back home has come to a stop. For him, every custom, every catchphrase, every ritual is reverently preserved. In this Sleeping Beauty homeland, childhood friends, unchanged of course, still mourn our departure, billboards still advertise the same brands. Ovid compares his death in exile to that of the dying swan uttering its final notes amidst the surrounding silence. "My own death shall be like this," he says, "but I myself shall perform my last rites."

Cortázar, who left Buenos Aires for Paris in 1951, once said that exile was the best way of ensuring devotion to your country. Ovid: "As long as I'm in Tomis, I'll write complaints."

Tuesday

Charlotte comes looking for her cat. The cat has decided to make herself at home in our place. Every so often Charlotte comes and picks her up, but five minutes later the cat is back. She walks into the garden, tail in the air, yawns luxuriously and then curls up in a perfect circle inside an unused lavender pot, or decides to nap in the stone flower box and stretches out to the edges in a curiously precise rectangle.

Ancestors of Mole, Toad and Rat: archaeologists in Mexico have discovered Olmec artifacts carved more than 2,500 years ago, depicting speaking animals.

Still on the subject of exile: "To me literature is forever blowing a horn, singing about youth when youth is irretrievably gone, singing about your homeland when in the schizophrenia of the times you find yourself in a land that lies over the ocean, a land—no matter how hospitable and friendly—where your heart is not, because you landed on those shores too late." Josef Skvorecky in Toronto, writing on his beloved Czechoslovakia.

Wednesday

I notice that I hurry through Toad's adventures. In the chapter called "The Return of Ulysses" the reclaiming of Toad Hall from the weasels has a certain epic grandeur, but Toad behaves like a spoiled brat, and has about him more of sulky Achilles than of the subtle King of Ithaca.

On the other hand, I can read the chapter "The Piper at the Gates of Dawn" a hundred times. "So beautiful and strange and new! Since it was to end so soon, I almost wish I had never heard it. For it has roused a longing in me that is pain, and nothing seems worth while but just to hear that sound once more and go on listening to it for ever."

Pages like this take place without translation into meaning, swiftly, and then we are back in the realm of reasoning and understanding.

Sunday

Christmas preparations.

Friday

A friend gives me a reproduction of the "Map of the Wild Wood and Surroundings" that Shepard drew for the endpaper pages of Grahame's book.

Cookham Dene, on the Thames, is the setting for *The Wind in the Willows*. Here Grahame lived when he wrote the book, with his wife and their son, Alastair, known affectionately as Mouse. Apparently, *The Wind in the Willows* was first told to the four-year-old Alastair after "a bad crying fit on the night of his birthday," episode after episode, till midnight. Years later, Alastair was killed in Oxford, in an unexplained accident. Suddenly, the book becomes an elegy.

Among celebratory remains of wrapping paper and Christmas food, I see that *Le Monde* has a long article on the copyright of landscapes. After the sale of museum reproduction rights to multinational companies, local governments, administrative organizations and private landowners have begun to claim rights over certain "natural views." Monuments such as the Eiffel Tower can be photographed for free during the day, but the right to reproduce the lit symbol of Paris at night belongs to a private company. Among the examples of visual private property: the view from the cliffs of Cassis, near Marseilles; the boats on the beach of Collioure, in southern France; the Estuary of Trieux, in Brittany. Will a future Kenneth Grahame have to pay some large corporation for the use of his memories of Cookham Dene on the Thames?

In a folder I keep, marked "Odd Clippings": "On January 18, 1949, an American by the name of James T. Mangan filed a charter with the Cook County Recorder of Deeds, and under the state attorney's authority claimed ownership to the whole of space. After giving his vast territory the name of Celestia, Mr. Mangan notified all countries on earth of his claim, warned them not to attempt any trips to the moon, and petitioned the United Nations for membership."

Tuesday

Foul weather. Tomorrow is the beginning of 2003. We'll spend New Year's Eve at the small restaurant in nearby Lencloître, Le Champ de Foire. Last December 31, they drew back the curtains at midnight and set up a minuscule fireworks display for us. Perhaps they'll do it again this year.

In Toronto there will be snow now. We remember Christmas visits to Barbara Howard and Richard Outram, and the white garden outside their window, and Barbara's rich voice and strong, beautiful hands. Living in France, I know that you can feel utterly at home in a place that is not the one to which you feel the deepest attachment. (Mole would agree.)

2003

JANUARY

Tuesday

The dismantling after Christmas. My family (who, being Jewish, had no reason to keep Christmas) followed the tradition of putting away the holiday decorations by the morning after Twelfth Night; otherwise they would attract bad luck. We take down the ornaments and C. carries the tree in its pot out into the garden, where it will wait until spring to be replanted. The pleasurable sense of beginning, but not from scratch. Like rereading.

Trees and bushes are covered in caterpillar frost. I like these cold, blustery holidays. Until my twentieth birthday, Christmas signaled the beginning of summer: the long days in the garden of the rented country house in Buenos Aires, or on the beach in Uruguay, under the pine trees, reading and cycling week after week until the dreaded start of school in March. I recall the physical pleasure of coming to the end of my book and then daydreaming about the characters (if I liked them) for many days after, imagining their ongoing lives and other endings. Now it seems impossible to find such periods of long calm.

Last week I read Susan Coyne's *Kingfisher Days* and realized that we shared similar slow-paced childhood summers. This sentence, for instance: "Once a week the Moirs went into town in their canoe to exchange their library books."

Wednesday

Out of the blue, I receive a letter from Professor Isaías Lerner in New York. He was one of my several Spanish literature teachers in high school, certainly one of the best and most memorable. He saw a piece I had published and decided to get in touch, after all this time. I must have been fifteen when I attended his class. For a whole year we studied *El Lazarillo*, *La Celestina*, *El Libro del buen amor*, but never got to *Don Quixote* because Lerner would take us through the books in loving detail, more interested in depth than in quantity. I found out, however, that he was teaching *Don Quixote* to another class, and I would sneak in to listen. The following summer I took with me a two-volume edition of Cervantes's novel, and spent all three months in its company.

To follow the reading in class and to read the book on my own, under the trees, were two utterly different experiences. I remember, for instance, Lerner's careful commentary on Don Quixote's library, which the Curate and the Barber decide to wall up in order to prevent further madness. Alone, I was almost in tears when I read the description of the old knight getting out of bed and going to look for his books, and being unable to find the room in which he kept them. That was for me the perfect nightmare: to wake up and discover that the place in which I kept my books had vanished, making me feel that I no longer was who I thought I was. Gregor Samsa submits to the metamorphosis, to his loss of self; Don Quixote instead, in order to continue to be Don Quixote, bravely accepts the explanation that an evil enchanter has spirited his library away. By assuming the fantasy, he remains faithful to his imagined self.

When I returned to Buenos Aires for a year in 1973, the books I had left at home were no longer there.

Friday

Don Quixote wants to be a just man for his own sake, not out of obedience to human or divine laws. "Ah, Lord! Give me the strength and the courage / To look upon my heart and my body without disgust!" The prayer by Baudelaire sums up Don Quixote's ethics.

The Hassidic master Rabbi David of Lelov, who died in 1813: "The web of just acts holds the world together, making it golden." Don Quixote: "Sancho, my friend, know that I was born, by Heaven's will, in this our iron age, to be reborn in that of gold, or golden, as it is often called." For the Hassidim, the existence of the world is justified by thirty-six just men known as the Lamed Wufniks, for whose sake God does not annihilate the human race. Don Quixote sets out to act as a just man would act in a world whose main characteristic is injustice.

In the paper today, further indications that war in Iraq is unavoidable. An Iraqi friend asks, "What course of action is possible between the atrocities of Saddam, the extremism of religious leaders and the economic voracity of the United States? We have the choice of being beheaded, stoned or eaten alive."

Saturday

Reading *Don Quixote*, I'm distracted by the world Cervantes has recreated and pay little attention to the unfolding of the story. The landscape through which the two adventurers travel, their daily conflicts, their pain and grime and hunger and friendship are so powerfully real that I forget that they follow a narrative, and simply enjoy their company. I am less interested in what will happen next than in what is happening now. I sometimes feel the same reading Conrad or Thomas Mann, or the Sherlock Holmes stories.

Lionel Trilling: "All prose fiction is a variation on the theme of *Don Quixote.*" Only if, by "theme," he means the reality and truth of prose fiction.

My son, Rupert, tells me, once again, how difficult he finds it to hold out for what he believes in: to refuse buying this, subscribing to that. He is only twenty, and constantly tempted by offers of betrayal which he wants to resist. I imagine he feels like a chess player who wants to see where a move will ultimately lead but is able to foresee only the immediate consequences.

Don Quixote knows his acts will have consequences, even though these remain invisible to him. Macbeth's dilemma is that he wishes for acts without consequences—the only real impossibility.

I remember a friend in Buenos Aires telling me of a woman who had to sit one day in a café next to the man who had tortured her son. That is the consequence of Argentina's refusal to act justly. Will this ever change? Not until the impunity granted to the military murderers is lifted, since this infamous amnesty will endlessly invalidate any attempt to restore social order. No society can exist coherently without a functioning code of justice; it must be part of society's definition of itself, and its citizens must believe in it, whether they uphold it or not. And abide by the consequences.

For Juan José Saer, Don Quixote is an epic hero because he is uninterested in whether his mission of justice will succeed or fail. "This is the essential point that must be retained," says Saer; "that the clear or muddled awareness of the ineluctability of failure in every human enterprise, is something fundamentally opposed to the moral epic." Compare this to Stevenson's remark: "Our mission in life is not to succeed, but to continue to fail in the best of spirits."

Mysteriously, this faith in the ineluctability of justice survives even when the hero himself cannot carry it further; the faith then becomes contagious and infects others with just zeal. At the end of Part I of *Don Quixote*, when Sancho brings home his wounded master, there is no feeling of conclusion but, rather, a promise of new beginnings. To his wife's demands for a cape for herself and shoes for their children, Sancho answers with the hope of other rewards, rewards that he may acquire some future day, after further adventures. This may seem mere greed, but then, while Don Quixote lies dazed in his bed and his niece and housekeeper curse the guilty novels that have made their master mad, it is Sancho who picks up the knight's chivalrous ideal, telling his wife, "There is nothing better in the world for an honest man than to be the squire of a knight-errant in search of adventures."

Brilliant observation by Schelling in his 1809 *Philosophie der Kunst*: "The main idea in *Don Quixote* is the struggle of an ideal against the reality that dominates the entire book, in its most diverse variations. At first, it seems as if the knight and his ideal are defeated, but this is only an appearance, because what becomes manifest throughout the novel is the absolute triumph of that ideal."

Don Quixote as Lamed Wufnik.

Monday

I have to stop working on the diary in order to write a bread-and-butter piece for a certain publication.

Virginia Woolf on the impossibility of writing a 25,000-word story on commission: "I think I've proved that to be true in this way: the humiliation, that is the obstinate refusal of the brain to comply & one's drubbings, & re-writings, & general despondency, even for 2,000 words, make it not so much morally, as physically, intellectually a torture."

Humiliation of the trade: I ring up a magazine editor, for the sixth time, to request the payment now three months overdue. After yet more excuses, she asks, "Do you really need £100 so badly?"

Dorothy Parker: "The two most welcome words in the English language are 'Cheque Enclosed.'"

Evening

Icy rain. C. lights a fire and we listen to Tom Jobim playing Vinicius, a gift my publisher, Luiz Schwarcz, sent us from Brazil.

About generosity: Saint Martin, Bishop of Tours, the saint to whom our village church is dedicated, is celebrated for having cut his cape in two and given half to a freezing beggar. Don Quixote observes that it must have been winter, "otherwise the saint, who was so charitable, would have given him the whole." "No, that surely wasn't the case," Sancho answers. "Instead, he must have upheld the old proverb that says, 'The man in wisdom must be old, who knows in giving where to hold.'"

Friday

Something has been moving in the crawl space all night. It sounds too big to be a mouse, too small to be a cat. I sit up, listening to it. Then I go downstairs and, in the dark, watch the very last red glimmers in the fire die out. After fifteen minutes, I go back to bed. When I was in my twenties, I was able to sit (at a café table, for instance) for hours on end, neither reading nor talking, not even concentrating on anything. Now I find it very hard to sit and *do nothing*.

Petra von Morstein, "Before Evening":

> A day
> In which I don't wish to find anything.
> I should gather it up
> And keep it safe.

There is no wasted time in *Don Quixote*. Reading *Erec et Enide*, the twelfth-century novel by Chrétien de Troyes, I come upon the word *récréantise*, a word that seems to combine "relaxation" (*récréation*) with "haunted feeling" (*hantise*), and which the annotator defines as a sort of lassitude, weakness, negligence, lack of caring that is deemed a vice in the novels of chivalry.

Saturday

More on consequences:

There are revelations that are not meant for us. Tchouang-Tseu (who in the fourth century B.C. imagined the dreamer who dreams he is a butterfly and who, upon waking, no longer knows if he is a man who dreamt he was a butterfly or a butterfly who is now dreaming he is a man) wrote this story: The son of a poor family makes his living fishing for pearls. One day, he dives into the sea and emerges with a pearl worth a thousand gold pieces. Instead of congratulating him, his father orders him to take a stone and smash the pearl. He argues that a pearl worth a thousand gold pieces must be so rare that it could be found only in a chasm nine fathoms deep and under the chin of a black dragon. It therefore follows that the son has been able to take the pearl only because the dragon had fallen asleep. "O my son!" he concludes, "think of what would happen to you once the dragon woke up!"

Sunday

This morning, reacting to yet another LePen assembly in France, my French publisher, Hubert Nyssen (who fought in the Resistance), says, "We'll have to pull out the old rifles once again."

Misery in our time: according to *Le Monde*, 53 percent of the children of London live below the poverty line. What action, then? The common argument: helping one beggar won't alter the situation, won't eradicate the cause, won't change anything. But for Don Quixote there is no doubt that direct action *is* the answer. On his very first excursion as a knight, he hears cries of distress and sees a boy, naked from the waist up, tied to a tree and being flogged by his master. Don Quixote orders the man to stop: "Uncivil sir, it is unseemly that you should attack one who cannot defend himself; mount your steed, couch your lance, and I will make you see the cowardice of what you are now doing." The boy's master attempts to explain that he is punishing him for his carelessness, and not (as the boy claims) for demanding his wages. Undeceived, Don Quixote orders the man to untie the boy and pay him what he owes him; the man answers that for him to do so, the boy must accompany him home, since he does not have the money on him. The boy, foreseeing that he will once again be beaten when left alone with his master, begs the knight not to believe him. "He will not disobey me," Don Quixote answers. "It is enough for me to give my orders and he will surely respect them." Because justice, chivalrous justice, is for Don Quixote an immutable universal law, and he believes that breaking it will entail unthinkable universal catastrophes. But, as the reader suspects, as soon as Don Quixote turns and leaves, the master ties the boy to the tree again and beats him within an inch of his life.

Twenty-seven chapters later, when Don Quixote meets the boy again and wishes to prove to his companions the importance of knights-errant by telling them the story of the rescue, the boy answers that the outcome of the adventure was exactly contrary to the knight's intentions, and begs Don Quixote, if he ever finds him in trouble again, to leave him as he is and not attempt to save him. Sancho, giving the boy a piece of bread and cheese for the road, comments, "Take this, brother, for we are all affected in some part by your misfortune." Reasonably, the boy asks in what part it has affected Sancho. "In this part of cheese and bread I give you" is the answer, but that is only one version of the truth. The boy's misfortune, as Sancho intuits, affects us all, not in the physical pain, of course, not in the empty stomach and the flogged skin, but in the realization that injustice thrives and that we are (apparently) condemned to the impossibility of overcoming it.

André Gide on Gandhi's assassination: "It is as if God had been defeated."

The chapter ends with the boy cursing his rescuer and all knights-errant, with Don Quixote sad and ashamed and his companions holding back their laughter at the scene they have witnessed.

I can no longer watch scenes of violence on television or in films, but I can read their fictional descriptions. *Don Quixote* is one of the most violent books I know.

Monday

Don Quixote presents itself as a bewildering set of Chinese boxes. After only three chapters, Cervantes tells us that he has got this far and now realizes that he no longer knows how the adventures of his knight continue. By chance, he is offered for sale a bundle of old papers; being a compulsive reader who reads "even torn scraps in the street," he leafs through them and sees that they are written in Arabic. Curious as to what these pages may contain, he seeks out a translator (Hebrew and Arab translators are easy to find even after their expulsion from Spain, Cervantes tells us), and discovers that the manuscript is nothing less than the chronicle of the adventures of Don Quixote, written by the Arab historian Cide Hamete Benegeli—who, it turns out, includes Cervantes among the authors in our knight's library. From then on, the spiral of authorship becomes vertiginous: the novel we read purports to be a translation from the Arabic, and Cervantes becomes not its "father" but merely its "godfather." Later, in Part II of *Don Quixote*, the characters have read Part I and correct and revise its factual errors, even though, Cervantes tells us, its Moorish author swears that all the events are true, "even as a Catholic Christian might swear" (which, the translator explains to Cervantes, means that he swears nothing but the truth). At this point, the reader wonders: who is inventing whom?

Most writers possess a historical presence; not so Cervantes, who, in my memory, is less a real man than a character in *Don Quixote*. Goethe, Melville, Jane Austen, Dickens, Nabokov are more or less recognizable writers of flesh and blood; Cervantes seems to me invented by his book.

In May of last year, with Javier Cercas, I visited Cervantes's house in Valladolid. The house is impressive. Here Cervantes lived when Part I of *Don Quixote* appeared in Madrid in 1605. The garden, the study, the bedroom, the room in which the many women of the family gathered around a Moorish coal-burner, the kitchen, which he no doubt seldom visited—all these (we agreed) held more of the world of Don Quixote than of his creator. In spite of museums like this one, in spite of the reputation, the monuments, the literature courses, the institutes named after him, the enthusiasm of posterity and the generosity of curators, Cervantes remains unreal.

Proust felt he was condemned to be the fictional "I" he had created. In *Don Quixote* it is as if the fictional "I" were condemned to be Cervantes.

Sancho and Don Quixote compared to Dr. Jekyll and Mr. Hyde: Nicholas Rankin, in his admirable travel book *Dead Man's Chest,* observes that "perhaps it is no accident that the letter of the alphabet between H for Hyde and J for Jekyll is I."

I found an engraving professing to be the portrait of Cide Hamete Benegeli. I've had it framed and have hung it on the wall next to my desk.

Later

Subjects dealt with weakly by Cervantes in many of his other works mysteriously come to life in *Don Quixote*. Compare the tedious enumeration of good and bad poets in his *Voyage to Parnassus* (a kind of pedestrian *commedia* in which the author's purpose seems to be merely to receive the approval of Apollo for his own poetic manifesto) to the book burners' census in *Don Quixote*.

Books within the book: when the Curate and the Barber ransack Don Quixote's collection in order to purge it of "evil" books, they come across *La Galatea* by a certain Miguel de Cervantes. "This Cervantes has been a great friend of mine for many years," says the Curate, "and I know he is more experienced in misfortune than in verses. His book has some good invention; it proposes something, and concludes nothing." Regarding *La Galatea*, "concludes nothing" simply means that Cervantes never wrote the second part. But the same could be said of *Don Quixote*, and for a stronger reason: *Don Quixote* "concludes nothing" because the physical death of the hero is not the conclusion of the ethical argument.

Flaubert: "Yes, stupidity consists in the desire to conclude."

Note: Flaubert could not have liked *Don Quixote*, written, as it is, without any visible effort to rein in the story or to master the prose. In a letter to a friend, Flaubert insists, "The weak passages in a book should be better written than the others."

Tuesday

Don Quixote tells Cardenio that he has "more than three hundred books" back home. Cervantes's books (and books on Cervantes) occupy three shelves in my own library. I notice that I still have the book on Cervantes that Javier Cercas insisted on lending me. I must send it back. I feel uncomfortable having other people's books at home. I want either to steal them or to return them immediately. There is something of the visitor who outstays his welcome in borrowed books. Reading them and knowing that they don't belong to me gives me the feeling of something unfinished, half enjoyed. This is also true of library books.

What would happen if the Curate and the Barber purged my library of memoirs and diaries the way they purged Don Quixote's of novels of chivalry?

"Saint Augustine's *Confessions*: I've heard say that this was the first book of memoirs, and that all others have their origin in this one, so as the law-giver of such a pernicious sect, it should be thrown into the fire."

"No, sir, because I've also heard say that it is the best of all books composed in this genre, and being unique of its kind it should be spared."

"The *Letters* of Madame de Sévigné: brilliant and lively, therefore keep. Rousseau's *Confessions*: maudlin, chuck away. Goethe's *Dichtung und Wahrheit*: half engaging, half presumptuous, tear it down the middle and keep the better half."

"Bioy Casares's diaries: they should have been ruthlessly pruned. Two things toll the death knell for such books, confessions of erotic seductions and descriptions of dreams. The first read as lecherous bragging; the second as painfully dull. Guilty of the first: Cellini's *Autobiography*, Casanova's *Journals*, Frank Harris's *My Life and Loves*. Guilty of the second, Graham Greene's *A World of My Own*. Out with all of them."

"Let us move quickly through this section; we can't stop at every single title. Amiel's *Diary*: too long. Prokosch's *Voices*: name-dropping and delusional. Strindberg's *Son of a Servant*: self-pitying and complacent. Neruda's *I Confess I Have Lived*: self-aggrandizing. All condemned."

"Wait now, what do we have here? The most perfect journal of all: Kafka's. Set it next to Saint Augustine; they should be honored in just the same way. Now, a few other respectable exceptions: the journals of Katherine Mansfield,

Virginia Woolf, Julien Green. All these, my friend, are intimate, wise and revealing; you must preserve them carefully. Cesare Pavese's *This Business of Living*: place it beside the previous three. And these? Two moving Canadian memoirs: Sharon Butala's *Wild Stone Heart* and Wayne Johnston's *Baltimore's Mansion*, both exactly right, each in its own way. Keep all six on the same shelf. One more: Hermann Broch's *Autobiographical Writings*, a uniquely conceived, intelligent memoir, mysteriously unknown in Germany."

"And this thing here, *A Reading Diary*, no less? Into the fire, don't you think?"

"Hold on! The author is a friend of mine, and even though the volume carries little grace and less intelligence, it has the merit of being enthusiastic and short, the latter thankfully atoning for the former. Spare it for now; later we shall see."

"Later! I'm not certain how much longer I can carry on with all this wallowing. All these first persons are becoming less singular by the minute. Bless me, what a lot of true-life stories! You would think we had enough unbidden confessions daily without deciding to pen more! How we enjoy the sound of our own voice!"

Auden, quoting an Icelandic proverb: "Every man enjoys the smell of his own farts."

Wednesday

Idiocy in academia seems to have no limits. Amherst College in Massachusetts has decided to offer a course in Espanglish—that is to say, in the mixture spoken by Latin American immigrants who have not yet learned English. Among the assignments, the translation of *Don Quixote.* These are the first two sentences: "In a placete de La Mancha of which nombre no quiero remembrearme, vivía, not so long ago, uno de esos gentlemen who always tienen una lanza in the rack, una buckler antigua, a skinny caballo y un grayhound para el chase. A cazuela with más beef than mutón, carne choppeada para la dinner, un omlet pa los sábados, lentil pa los viernes, y algún pigeon como delicacy especial pa los domingos, consumían tres cuarers de su income."

Yesterday, in Nigeria, Islamic protesters rioted after hearing that the Miss World contest would take place in their country. They set fire to churches and shops belonging to Catholics and wounded or killed more than five hundred people, stabbing them with knives or placing burning tires around their necks. They ran down the streets of Kaduna shouting, "God is great!" and "Down with beauty!"

Thursday

If I had to choose a favorite passage in the novel, I think it would be the episode of Clavileño, when Don Quixote and Sancho are tricked into mounting, with their eyes covered, a wooden horse that supposedly will take them through the air to visit the wizard Malambruno. If they are indeed flying, Sancho asks, how is it that they can still clearly hear the voices of those on earth? Don Quixote dismisses the question as simply another peculiarity of their magical business. Sancho then suggests that they at least peek from under their blindfolds to see where they are. And it is then that Don Quixote shows how ambiguous his supposed delusion is: he forbids Sancho to remove his blindfold.

Faith must not be subject to the proofs of reason. Faith does not battle reason; it simply asserts itself by creating a place of emptiness for itself. It is into this emptiness, mystics believe, that God can enter.

Friday

Leave for Canada to give a lecture at the University of Newfoundland.

Saturday

My first visit to St. John's, Newfoundland. Immediately, the sense of being in an alien place, an island world with its own rules, its own language, its own imagination. I add St. John's to the places where I think I could live happily.

This evening a blizzard broke out over the city. From my hotel room, which has two huge corner windows, I see the snow clouds blow in and shatter endlessly against the glass, as if the whole building were swimming into waves of white.

Four of the most memorable weather experiences in my life have happened in Canada: this blizzard; the northern lights in Manitoba; a tornado in Saskatchewan; a storm coming up from the Pacific, seen from the librarian's house perched on a cliff above Campbell River, British Columbia.

Weather is a Canadian subject. There is no weather to speak of in *Don Quixote*.

Wednesday

Back home to France. Rain and mist. The cat has climbed up on the pigeon tower, and watches the puddles in the garden from a box lined with towels.

Dante wants us to believe in the beauty of Beatrice, so perfect that her place is in Heaven. Catullus and Petrarch try to convince us of the many attractions of their beloveds. Don Quixote attempts no such arguments. When the merchants whom he meets on his first outing ask that he show them a portrait of Dulcinea before they swear to her unparallelled beauty, he answers, "If I were to show her to you, what would be the merit of your confessing such a notorious truth? The importance of my demand consists in your believing, acknowledging, affirming upon oath and defending her beauty before you have seen it."

Perhaps the great literary characters are those few who will always escape our full understanding. The unbearable Lear bringing his hundred cronies to his daughter's house, the love-dejected

Dante obsessed by a young girl he has met only briefly, the trouble-prone, delusional Don Quixote beaten and stoned for persisting in his delusions—why do they move us to tears, why do they haunt us, why do they intimate that this life makes sense after all, in spite of everything? They offer no reason; they demand that we believe, acknowledge, affirm their existence, "upon oath."

FEBRUARY

Saturday

Similar to other "end of the world" places—Finisterre, Land's End, Tierra del Fuego—Newfoundland has the quality of standing outside ordinary time. St. John's has something of the Fort in Dino Buzzati's novel *The Tartar Steppe* (which I reread on my return flight): a place that seems impossible to leave but also impossible to reach, a place so anchored in its own routine that nothing from the outside can touch it. Maybe that is why I found St. John's so appealing.

Favorite cities:

- Venice
- Hobart
- Madrid
- Edinburgh
- Bologna
- Istanbul
- Poitiers
- Sélestat
- Oslo

- Bogotá
- Tiradentes
- Algiers
- St. John's

Like so many of my favorite books, Buzzati's is one that I first read during my adolescence: the story of Drogo, a young man posted to "the Fort" on the edge of the so-called Tartar Steppe, who over the years becomes obsessed with proving himself a soldier in battle with the never-materializing Tartars. The Fort is an uneasy haven; a complicated system of passwords controls its entry and exit. I remember feeling (I feel it again now) the terror of being caught in Drogo's nightmare of daily secrets—secrets entrusted to only one commanding officer, who might lose his memory or his way. The web of absurd rules and the threat of an invisible enemy echoed then all the frustrations and helplessness of adolescence; now it echoes all the frustrations and helplessness of more-than-middle age.

Buzzati's Fort exists within the concentric circles of its own rituals; it is a magical place that locks out time. It is not that time has stopped here but that, even more horribly, it continues at its own pace, distancing the Fort from the rest of the cosmos. In a place like this, everything inside you wants to move away; everything outside you keeps you back.

There is a memorable passage in the sixth chapter, describing Drogo in his sleep, dreaming of the seemingly never-ending journey to the Fort, which he cannot imagine. "Is it far yet? No, you have to cross the river down below there, climb those green hills . . . Another ten miles—people will say—just over that river and you'll be there. Instead you never reach the end." I wonder if this is what Alejandra Pizarnik (who certainly had read the novel) had in mind when she wrote that poem I love remembering: "And it is always the garden of lilies on the other bank of the river. If the soul asks, is it far? you shall answer: on the other bank of the river, not this one but that."

Sunday

Compared to the rain in Newfoundland, the winter rain in France feels warm.

Drogo needs to believe that the Tartars exist and that they pose a threat, so that he can long for the chance to fight them. He needs to believe in the Enemy.

In the paper last week: against the decision of the United Nations, eight European leaders have given their signed approval to Bush—including Vaclav Havel, whom I so admired. Maybe, now that the Communist threat has vanished, he needs to believe in some other Enemy.

Buzzati and Kafka (1): perhaps it is not only impossible to achieve justice. Perhaps we have even made it impossible for a just man to persevere in seeking justice.

Drogo is aware that time will not stop, that time in the Fort is made of consecutive present moments and that he is a different man in each of those moments. In one of these he wishes he had never come, in another he accepts his condition, in yet a third he hopes he will be a warrior on the battlefield, in a fourth he realizes that none of these present moments will continue to be "now." He describes his mother's attempt "to preserve the time of his childhood" by shutting up his room, and adds, "She was mistaken in believing that she could keep intact a certain state of happiness which had vanished for ever, that she could hold back the flight of time, that if she reopened doors and windows when her son returned, things would be as before."

My first sense of time passing: age six or seven, returning to our house after the holidays and finding that not *everything* was exactly the same.

On the flight back from St. John's I made these lists:

On the theme of time suspended:

- Bioy Casares, "The Perjury of the Snow"
- James Hilton, *Lost Horizon*
- Kobo Abe, *Woman in the Dunes*
- Perrault, "Sleeping Beauty"
- Washington Irving, "Rip Van Winkle"
- Alfonso el Sabio, the fable of the singing bird that makes a hundred years seem like a few minutes, in *Las Partidas*

On places that cannot be left:

- Léon Bloy, "The Captives of Longjumeau"
- Buñuel, *The Exterminating Angel*
- Sartre, *Huis Clos*
- Hans Christian Andersen, "The Snow Queen"
- Tennyson, "The Lotus-Eaters"

On places that cannot be reached:

- Lord Dunsany, "Carcassonne"
- André Dhôtel, *Le pays où l'on n'arrive jamais*
- Sir Thomas Bulfinch, *My Heart's in the Highlands*
- Book of Genesis, the Promised Land (for Moses)
- Kurt Weill, "Youkali"
- Kafka, *The Castle*

Buzzati notes that, from the very beginning of his writing career, people heard Kafka's echoes in his work. As a consequence, he said, he felt not an inferiority complex but "an annoyance complex." And as a result, he lost any desire to read Kafka's work.

Monday

I've just discovered that Lord Byron's dog, Boatswain (for whom he composed a moving epitaph), was born in Newfoundland.

Tuesday

The passwords to get in and out of the Fort are contingent on time. Because they change daily, any soldier who forgets them is in danger of being left outside forever. Coded words must regulate every soldier's existence. The coded language of the military, the conventional language of war, attempts to posit the world in an arbitrary and clear-cut context. Without it, conflict would be impossible.

Buzzati's method of passwords joins Bush's vocabulary of unambiguous terms: good and evil, them and us, black and white, right and wrong. In the twelfth-century *Chanson de Roland: "Païens ont tort et Chrétiens ont droit."*

Ernest Bramah, in *Kai Lung's Golden Hours*: "It is scarcely to be expected that one who has spent his life beneath an official umbrella should have at his command the finer analogies of light and shade."

Sunday

War seems at the same time imminent and yet impossible. The view of the conflict offered by the European newspapers is merely allegorical: American power in the shape of a willful monster attacking other monsters. Since we don't believe in dragons, the allegory is useless. An editorial in the London *Daily Telegraph* tells us that the "World Economy requires the War Machinery." We are in the realm of ornamental capital letters.

Ron Wright called this morning from Port Hope. He argues that Bush's bully tactics mark "the end of democracy." I agree. But I wonder whether we can ever witness such titled events on a huge scale ("The Fall of the Roman Empire," "The Conquest of America," "The Holocaust") or whether we are always left with a tiny corner of the picture from which, in the best cases, we can intuit the whole. It may be that we have to resign ourselves to dealing in details.

Voltaire: "Curse the details, posterity is blind to them all."

The suspect intentions of all sides in this conflict make it difficult to consider it with any clarity. One would require Buzzati's ability to maintain coherence in the midst of constantly shifting points of view. For Buzzati, even the reader's perspective must be brought into the story, since we, too, must be made responsible for the events. "Look how small they are," Buzzati tells us, pointing at Drogo and his horse, "how small against the side of the mountains, which are growing higher and wilder."

The looming war has nothing heroic about it; we know that the motives driving the Anglo-American forces are less humanitarian than financial. In Buzzati's story, on the other hand, the tragic feeling of absurdity that overcomes the reader stems largely from the utter futility of the heroic enterprise. No humanitarian or financial reasons can be invoked. The frontier gives no trouble, the Tartar Steppe has not seen Tartars in living memory, the heroes are never granted the chance of being heroic.

DROGO: "So the Fort has never been of any use whatsoever?"

THE CAPTAIN: "None at all."

Someone told me this joke: Moishe meets his friend Jacob on the way out of their shtetl. "I'm leaving for America," says Jacob. "Soon I'll be far away." Moishe: "Far away from what?"

Monday

Brilliant sunshine, crisp cold. My neighbor comes over with a gift of fresh eggs and stays for twenty minutes discussing the conflict in Iraq. How strange for an Iraqi farmer half a world away, if he were to know that his fate is the subject of a conversation here, in a small, almost invisible French village.

Looking at the soldier who supplies him with the rules and laws governing the passwords, Drogo wonders what is left of him after twenty-two years in the Fort. "Did [he] still remember that somewhere there existed millions of men like himself who were not in uniform? Men who moved freely about the city and at night could go to bed or to a tavern or to the theatre, just as they liked?"

"The eye with which I see God is the same eye with which God sees me," noted Meister Eckhart.

Wednesday

From an apocryphal book of devotions: "God reveals in utter clarity that which we can't understand; that which we *can* understand He lays out in riddles."

I have often had this idea: that the (false) impression of being able to see in front of us the entire chart of action, the totality of a situation, leads us to believe that other choices are open to us. I say to myself, "I am sitting here, in my room, writing, but I could be elsewhere, doing something quite different," which is like saying, "I could lead another life, I could be someone else."

Buzzati and Kafka (2): Drogo is seized by the unfulfillable desire to escape. "Why had he not left at once? . . . Why had he given in?" Drogo's questions reaffirm the ineluctability of his condition. He can imagine escaping only because it is impossible. Kafka in his *Diaries*: Should I greatly yearn to be an athlete, it would probably be the same thing as my yearning to go to heaven and to be permitted to be as despairing there as I am here."

In the ninth-century *Life and Times of Pai Chu-yi*: "Walking towards the scaffold, Li Tzu turned to his son with these words: 'Ah, if we were in Shanghai, hunting hares with our white hound!'"

Later

I note that the philosopher John Rawls, who died last year, has been remembered by his publishers with this quotation:

> The perspective of eternity is not a perspective from a certain place beyond the world, nor the point of view of a transcendent being; rather it is a certain form of thought and feeling that rational persons can adopt within the world. And having done so, they can, whatever their generation, bring together into one scheme all individual perspectives and arrive together at regulative principles that can be affirmed by everyone as he lives by them, each from his own standpoint. Purity of heart, if one could attain it, would be to see clearly and to act with grace and self-command from this point of view.

The Palestinian poet Mahmoud Darwish: "I am myself alone an entire generation."

Thursday

My friends Gottwalt and Lucie sent me a magnificent illustrated book on the "Dance of Death" in the Marienkirche in Lübeck, which we visited together a year ago. Against an unremarkable landscape of cities, ports and countryside, every one of society's members is carried away in a macabre chorus line, linking arms with skeletons draped in shrouds. The ordinary atmosphere seems to contradict the monstrosity of death; in fact, it grounds it in our daily business, a reminder of what we carry within. That reminder is present all along in Buzzati's work.

Buzzati in his notebooks: "All writers and artists, however long they live, say only one same thing."

In "The Death of Ivan Illich," Tolstoy describes Ivan's progress toward death as being on a train and having the sudden impression of traveling in the opposite direction, and then being proven wrong. This is the feeling I have throughout *The Tartar Steppe*, that I am afforded the description not so much of a long death as of a sleep that sometimes resembles wakefulness.

Death and his brother, Sleep: the first version of this image I find in the *Epic of Gilgamesh*, 2000 B.C.: "The sleeping and the dead, how alike they are, like painted death."

The Tartar Steppe suggests a familiarity with death. I suspect that, in spite of the hundreds of deaths we see every week on our television screens, we have become utterly unfamiliar with it. We hide our dying in hospitals and retirement homes, and we make believe that we step from being there to not being there with no transition, as if the screen went suddenly blank. We make no allowance for passage.

I think the skulls that medieval scholars kept on their desks as memento mori were useful acknowledgments of something we will become but that we already carry within us. I'm not sure why we speak of transformation when we refer to dying; we don't change, we merely expose the dust within.

Henri Michaux: "Man, his essential being, is but a speck. It is this speck that death devours."

The newspaper today describes the work of a German surgeon turned artist who exhibits cadavers of humans and animals in various positions. Apparently, several people have offered to donate their bodies for him to use after their death. Now the surgeon has announced that he will perform a dissection publicly, as a performance piece. The banality of such an exhibition is astonishing. It is that very banality of his use of the dead that renders this man's work obscene.

Tomás Eloy Martínez told me that the actress Norma Aleandro was once visiting a ranch somewhere in Patagonia. The wealthy landowners, proud of their property, displayed for her many of their treasures: valuable paintings, ceramics, books. Encouraged by Aleandro's polite enthusiasm, her hosts said they would show her their favorite piece, and put a small copy of Goethe's poems in her hand. Aleandro commented on the soft, delicately tooled binding. "Yes, that's it," they said. "It's bound in human skin."

I loved someone who died. The last time I was with him, death made him look as if he had woken up in the past, magically young, as he had once been when he was without experience of the world, and happy because he knew that everything was still possible.

Sunday

A cold, crisp, sunny day.

A friend who has been writing a novel for the past eight years is afraid of finishing it. Draft after draft, revision after revision, she postpones the day of handing it over to the publisher, knowing of course that, once it is printed, all hope of its resembling the novel in her mind will be extinguished, and she will be left with the reality of a creation independent from her will and her desire.

Buzzati and Kafka (3): Drogo hears the news that a battalion of Tartars may at last be approaching the Fort. Feeling too weak to fight, he tells himself that the news will prove mistaken. "He hoped that he might not see anything at all, that the road would be deserted, that there would be no sign of life. That was what Drogo hoped for after wasting his entire life waiting for the enemy."

Wednesday

I finished *The Tartar Steppe* yesterday. The last pages are astonishing. I walk in the garden as they echo in my mind. The cat follows me.

When Drogo dies (as an old man, with his wish to fight the Tartars unfulfilled), Buzzati is there to console him. At the death of Don Quixote, Cervantes finds no words to take leave of his friend, his creation or his creator, and can only stammer, "His spirit departed; I mean to say, he died." At Drogo's death, Buzzati tells his creature that there is still another, better fight waiting for him, not against Tartars, not against "men like himself who were tortured as he was by longing and by suffering, with flesh that one could wound, with faces one could look into," but against "a being both evil and omnipotent." And Buzzati has this to add: "Be brave, Drogo, this is your last card—go to death like a soldier and at least allow your mistaken life to end well. Finally take your revenge on fate; no one will sing your praises, no one will call you a hero or anything like that; but for that very reason it is worth the effort. Step across the shadow line with a firm step, erect as if on parade, and, if you can, even smile. After all, your conscience is not too heavy, and God will certainly grant you pardon."

At the hour of my death, these are the lines I would like to remember.

MARCH

Monday

I note that Hervé Guibert bought Rilke's *Letters to a Young Poet* in order to read the same book at the same time as his lover, who was away traveling.

Coincidences (even those created artificially), a chance encounter with a friend I have not seen for a long time, the taste of apricots, the discovery of a book I have been searching for, the light at dusk at this time of year, the sound of the wind in the chimney, utter quiet and darkness before falling asleep: all these are for me unexpected moments of happiness. But there are other happy moments attached to nothing: to no event, no particular thought, no pleasing sensation. A feeling utterly ignorant of its causes, silent and sudden and overwhelming.

It was Silvina Ocampo who first told me to read *The Pillow Book* of Sei Shonagon. "You'll like it," she said, "because you like making lists."

The edition I now have of Sei Shonagon's book (I lost the copy Silvina gave me) has an introduction by Ivan Morris, the English translator, explaining that, in medieval Japan, a pillow book was simply a notebook stored away in the drawer of a wooden pillow. It contained personal observations, gossip, impressions of daily events and, above all, lists. Sei Shonagon's *Pillow Book* contains 164 lists. I pick it up now, thinking what a perfect book it is to read at a time of fragmentation.

According to Novalis, after the Fall Paradise was scattered in fragments all over the Earth. That is why it is now so difficult to find.

I realize that I think in fragments. When I think of Silvina, what I hold in my memory is a composite portrait made up of images and snatches of conversation of varying degrees of intensity, torn from their context or transformed through retelling and forgetting. I remember her husky, tremulous voice on the phone, her large spidery handwriting, the dark glasses that hid her eyes because she thought her face was not attractive, the book-lined apartment she shared with Bioy Casares. I remember her sitting with her beautiful legs tucked under her in the armchair, inventing games for her guests, reading out loud her stories and poems.

About Sei Shonagon's book I remember Silvina saying, "How nice not to have to worry about a beginning or an ending."

Sei Shonagon was lady-in-waiting to the empress of Japan during the last years of the tenth century. Her contemporary, Murasaki Shikibu—author of the world's first psychological novel, *The Tale of Genji*—had this to say about her: "She is a gifted woman, to be sure. Yet if one gives free rein to one's emotions even under the most inappropriate circumstances, if one has to sample each interesting thing that comes along, people are bound to regard one as frivolous. And how can things turn out well for such a woman?"

Jane Austen, in one of her letters: "I do not want people to be very agreeable, as it saves me the trouble of liking them a great deal."

Tuesday

Like close-ups in documentary films, brief sketches in books of memoirs suddenly give a sense of immediacy to the writing. Chateaubriand is a master of this device.

Sei Shonagon, giving an example of "People Who Looked Pleased with Themselves": "A man who has received the governorship of one of the first-class provinces that is being offered in the current period of official appointments. 'What a splendid appointment!' people say and congratulate him warmly, to which he smugly replies, 'How so? I've been ruined.'"

I've noticed that women who observe things closely seem to make men uneasy. Schiller writes to Goethe about the observant Mme de Staël: "She wants to explain, to understand, to measure everything, she accepts nothing obscure, unfathomable, and for her nothing exists that cannot be illuminated by her torch." And he concludes, "She hasn't the slightest feeling for that which we call poetry."

Though much of Sei Shonagon's social life appears to be conducted through plotting, scheming, flattering the empress and gossip, her writing never resembles that of a tabloid columnist or a scandalmonger. Her descendants are John Aubrey, Jane Austen, Ivy Compton-Burnett and Barbara Pym. "If I am really close to someone, I realize that it would be hurtful to speak badly about him and when the opportunity for gossip arises I hold my peace. In all other cases, however, I freely speak my mind and make everyone laugh."

Thursday

A thin, irresolute drizzle. The cat sits on the step at the entrance of my writing room and watches the flooded garden. I read to it out loud this passage in *The Pillow Book*: "When you have gone away and face the sun that shines so crimson in the East, be mindful of the friends you left behind, who in this city gaze upon the endless rains."

It's my birthday. I'm suddenly fifty-five years old. Victor Hugo tells how Pope Pius IX met with Hugo's nephew Jules and asked him how old his uncle was. "Fifty-five," Hugo's nephew answered. "Alas!" exclaimed the pope. "He is too old to return to the Church."

For many years now, I have always sat down to write something (even one sentence will do) on March 13. I have the feeling that if I put down a few words, the act will somehow color the year ahead and I will not feel empty. Then, shreds of routine: preparing lunch, a nap, reading the paper.

I imagine a "sentimental library" made up of books I'd like to have for purely anecdotal reasons:

- Alice Liddell's copy of *Alice's Adventures in Wonderland*
- The Boileau that Gide read while sailing down the Congo

- Saint Augustine's Cicero
- The copy of *Leaves of Grass* that Walt Whitman gave to his lover, Peter Doyle
- Keats's Chapman's *Homer*
- Wallace Stevens's annotated copy of Keats's *Poems*
- Averroës' Aristotle
- The copy of "The Metamorphosis" that Kafka gave to his father
- Rimbaud's *Une saison en enfer* given to his teacher Georges Izambard
- Mishima's copy of *Une saison en enfer*
- Akhmatova's *Dante*, annotated in her hand
- John Gielgud's copy of *The Tempest*
- The *Amadís* that belonged to Cervantes
- The copy of Heine's *Poems* that Borges used to learn German
- Freud's copy of *Gentlemen Prefer Blondes*

Later

Bush and Blair refuse to listen to the demands for more time from the chief weapons inspector, Hans Blix. It becomes increasingly obvious that the Anglo-Americans no longer require an excuse for the war.

Sei Shonagon: "There are times when the world so exasperates me that I feel I cannot go on living in it for another moment and I want to disappear for good. But then, if I happen to obtain some nice white paper, Michinoku paper, or white decorated paper, I decide that I can put up with things as they are a little longer."

Saturday

Life in tenth-century Japan was excruciatingly monotonous for the women at the imperial court. Subjected to meticulous rituals of appropriateness, they could do little more than glimpse, from time to time, the goings-on in the world of men. They were restricted to certain quarters, expected to move, eat and speak in certain prescribed ways, and while the accepted language of the court was Chinese, women were taught only Japanese, which was thought unfit for serious literature.

In such a context, I wonder whether lines like the following, describing male activities, should be read ironically: "It is delightful when a man on horseback recites poetry at dawn."

What tone should we lend to a text written ten centuries ago, in a language we cannot read, by a woman whose circumstances are perhaps beyond our imagination?

I find it curious that sometimes the words fall precisely into place as I follow a thought in my writing, as if, in the unraveling of that thought, shapes and sounds returned to a pre-established order that seems exactly right. It is as if the words were clustered from the very beginning into a shape that, from a distance, I can only vaguely make out, and which, as I approach it, reveals itself fully formed, distinct and apprehensible. On such occasions, it is as if writing consisted in seeing clearly something that was there from the start.

Ivan Morris notes that tenth-century Japanese used repetition as a deliberate stylistic device: what to an English or Spanish ear may sound clumsy becomes in Japanese "a sort of poetic refrain." A warning to literal translators who, in attempting to reconstruct a text word by word in another language, forget that not only the instrument but the sensibility of the listener is other.

In *The Pillow Book*, the choice of one right word will lend truth to an otherwise banal observation: "Moonlight makes me think of people who are far away."

On the other hand, the wrong word renders an original observation banal: "I have never come across anyone with such keen ears as Masamitsu, the minister of the Treasury. I believe he could hear the sound of a mosquito's eyelash falling on the floor."

The importance of the mot juste. Borges, on a trip to Portugal, asked a journalist who was interviewing him whether King Manoel II (on whom he had written a poem) was sixteen years old when he got lost in the North African desert. "No," answered the journalist, "the king was twenty-four when he disappeared." "Ah," said Borges, "then the adjective in the poem should not be *mágico desierto* (magical desert) but *místico desierto* (mystical desert)."

But even the right word will not repair a lame creation, as Don Quixote points out, recalling a certain artist who painted a rooster in such poor fashion and so badly depicted it that "he needed to write in capital letters next to it, *This is a rooster.*"

Sei Shonagon never needs to clarify anything.

Sunday

I receive a letter from Luiz Schwarcz in Brazil, telling me that he is thinking of editing a series on literary heroes and asking me which ones I would choose. My list is not as long as I imagined:

- Alice
- Sancho
- Lord Jim
- Prince Florizel of Bohemia
- Wakefield
- Mr. Pond
- Peter Schlemihl
- Pinocchio

Sei Shonagon makes a list of what she considers "poetic subjects." The list itself reads like a poem:

> The capital city. Arrowroot. Water-bur. Colts. Hail. Bamboo grass. The round-leaved violet. Club moss. Water oats. Flat river-boats. The mandarin duck. The scattered *chigaya* reed. Lawns. The green vine. The pear tree. The jujube tree. The althea.

There is a certain magical arbitrariness to list-making, as if sense were to be created by association alone.

Sei Shonagon lists "Things that give an unclean feeling":

A rat's nest.
Someone who is late in washing his hands in the morning.
White snivel, and children who sniffle as they walk.
The containers used for oil.
Little sparrows.
A person who does not bathe for a long time even though the weather is hot.
All faded clothes . . . especially those that have glossy colours.

Seneca's father asked Albucius Silus (first century) for examples of unclean subjects (*sordidissima*). He answered, "Rhinoceroses. Latrines. Sponges. Pets. Adulterous people. Food. Death. Gardens."

Saddam Hussein wrote a novel under a pseudonym, but everyone in Iraq knew who the real author was. An Iraqi journalist exiled since 1999 in Berlin told me that, after Saddam's henchmen had ransacked his house, killed his father and brother and beaten him until he was almost unconscious, one of the men placed Saddam's novel by his side, telling him that now he could try reading "something good for a change."

Monday

The scraps of news about the imminent war alternate with long, insignificant television images showing monotonous desert landscapes and blurred military gatherings. Zapping through the channels, I am gripped by a nauseating feeling of incoherence, of fragments whose lack of meaning stems not from the fact that they are fragments but from the fact that they belong to an incoherent whole. In the aftermath of the two world wars, the myriad voices denouncing, explaining, crying out and warning of the future may have sounded incomprehensible only as long as the framework was ignored. Today, the fragments merely echo a general state of incoherence. No attempt is made to disguise the folly, no excuses are proposed for absurd actions. (George Bush, Sr.: "I never apologize for the United States.") Protests against the war, arguments based on international law, demands for explanations, reports of official committees, facts and figures published in the papers are all stripped of meaning by the lunatic speech of those in power.

I suggest compiling *A Pillow Book for World Leaders*, to be distributed gratis at summit gatherings. I contribute two quotations:

From the fourth canto of Camões's *Lusiads*: "Oh, the folly of it, this craving for power, this thirsting after the vanity we call fame, this fraudulent pleasure known as honour that thrives on popular esteem! When the vapid soul succumbs to its lure, what a price it exacts, and how justly, in perils, tempests, torments, death itself! It wrecks all peace of soul and body, leads men to forsake and betray their loved ones, subtly yet undeniably consumes estates, kingdoms, empires. Men call it illustrious, and noble, when it merits instead the obloquy infamy; they call it fame, and sovereign glory, mere names with which the common people delude themselves on their ignorance."

From Erasmus's *In Praise of Folly*: "I am, as you can see, that true dispenser of good things, she whom the Latins called *Stultitia* (Stupidity) . . . I wear no make-up; I don't falsely twist my features to show a feeling my heart doesn't share. I am myself, so that even those who most strenuously display the mask and the name of Wisdom cannot disguise me; they carry on like monkeys dressed in purple and like donkeys in the skin of a lion."

Tuesday

Sei Shonagon is snobbish, venerates the imperial family, despises the lower classes, shows no interest in the lives of those outside the court. And yet her fragments acquire meaning for us, their future readers, outside their historical framework. We ignore the conventions that rule her daily transactions, her trains of thought, her displays of emotion, and yet we feel her observations to be true. For instance:

> "When one has stopped loving somebody, one feels that he has become someone else, even though he is still the same person."

In the *Tales of Ise*, a collection of prose and poetry written during the time of Sei Shonagon:

> Is not that the moon?
> And is not the spring the same
> Spring of the old days?
> My body is the same body
> Yet everything seems different.

In the newspaper: the global corporation NCR is financing research, at the University of Southern California, into a machine that will read and interpret the facial expressions of emotions.

Thursday

In spite of the United Nations' decision to the contrary, the Americans have begun to bomb Baghdad. On television, all that is shown is a continuous black screen with occasional bursts of light signifying missile hits.

Kafka to his friend Oskar Pollak, on Sunday, August 24, 1902: "I sat at my beautiful desk. You don't know it. How could you? It is namely a good bourgeois well-disposed desk, meant for teaching. It has, there where usually the writer's knees are, two frightful wooden points. And now pay attention. When one sits quietly, carefully, and writes something good and bourgeois, then one is fine. But woe if one becomes excited and twitches the body just a little, for then one inevitably gets the points in the knees and how it hurts. I could show you the dark blue marks. And what does that mean, then? 'Don't write anything exciting and don't allow your body to twitch.'"

Friday

It is curious how the books I choose to read at a certain moment often contradict the mood of that moment. Not stark oppositions, rather shifts of atmosphere.

Now I'm reading classic detective novels in which murder is given a reasonable setting. In *Surfacing*, Margaret Atwood has her narrator say of detective novels: "Cold comfort but comfort, death is logical, there's always a motive. Perhaps that's why she read them, for the theology."

Also, a collection of elegant essays by Stevenson, *Memoirs and Portraits*. And Stevenson tells me why: "Life is monstrous, infinite, illogical, abrupt, and poignant; a work of art, in comparison, is neat, finite, self-contained, rational, flowing and emasculate." This defines for me Sei Shonagon's book of fragments.

Sei Shonagon on reading: "Pleasing things: Finding a large number of tales that one has not read before. Or acquiring the second volume of a tale whose first volume one has enjoyed. But often it is a disappointment."

Marguerite Yourcenar: "Our true birthplace is that in which we cast for the first time an intelligent eye on ourselves. My first homelands were my books."

Sunday

A crisp, sunny day, intensely blue.

A wedding in our church. Most of the year, the church is empty: the village flock is not large enough to justify a weekly mass, so Saint Martin is used only for the occasional wedding or funeral. During the summer months, one of the villagers opens the doors in the morning and locks them toward seven o'clock in the evening, assuming that a stray visitor may be interested in inspecting it. She also looks after the bells, though they are now on an automatic tolling system. However, just before locking up, she sometimes enjoys ringing the bells by hand. She grabs hold of the rope and swings, the whole weight of her body jerking up and down as the deep, hollow peals echo throughout the ancient emptiness.

Sei Shonagon tells how the Governor of Ise visited her one day and found her pillow book on the veranda; in spite of her protests, he took it away with him and did not return it until much later. After that, her book was passed about in court. Did Sei Shonagon's fellow courtiers suspect that this woman's keen eye was granting them a minuscule form of immortality?

This morning, I looked at the books on my shelves and thought that they have no knowledge of my existence. They come to life because I open them and turn their pages, and yet they don't know that I am their reader.

APRIL

Friday

At dinner, my daughter Rachel asks me what I remember most about my father. I take a long moment to answer because I think what I remember most is his physique (he was a big, mustachioed, black-haired man), and I know that is not what she is asking. My children barely knew him, since he died almost twenty years ago, and I don't know what to tell her.

Curiously, for a long time now I have been dreaming about him: brief, episodic dreams whose relationship to one another I can't make out.

Two instances:

There is an avalanche of stones, somewhere that looks like a Wild West desert. The stones, huge and round and white, come rolling across the plain with a deafening rumble. I know I'll be caught in their path but I can't move. The stones hit me but instead of them hurting me, I myself become a stone. As I roll on with them, I notice that a larger stone rolling by my side is my father.

My father and I are having dinner at a restaurant. He smiles and caresses my face with the back of two fingers (as he used to do sometimes), and I'm thinking, "What will we talk about? What can I say that will interest him?" Suddenly the waiter, whose face I can't see, puts a covered silver dish in front of us. He takes the lid off, and there on the dish are the remains of a tiny charred mermaid, the skull visible through the leathery skin. I'm horrified. My father smiles, not noticing my horror.

I think he would have liked our house here in France. He would have enjoyed walking in the garden, especially now, in April, when you can see the beginning of the roses that C. trimmed back last year.

"Would he have come to visit you if he hadn't died?" Rachel asks.

Margaret Atwood, in *Surfacing*: "But nothing has died, everything is alive, everything is waiting to become alive."

Saturday

Surfacing was the first Canadian novel I read with the full awareness that it was Canadian. I had read Robertson Davies's *Deptford Trilogy*, and a memorable science-fiction novel, *A Strange Manuscript Found in a Copper Cylinder*, by James De Mille, as well as the Whiteoaks saga of Mazo de la Roche, which my father had in his library in a stammering Spanish translation—all without realizing that the authors were from Canada. Perhaps proof of how aleatory the concept of nationality is lies in the fact that we must learn it before we can recognize it as such. The concept of nationality is not self-evident, like the concepts of autobiography or fable-telling.

Surfacing is the story of a woman searching for her lost father in northern Quebec, and in the process surrendering herself to the natural world. The narrator's companions fumbling along in the bush, the member of the Wildlife Preservation Association who wants to buy her father's property, the francophones she meets during her quest—all seem to want to own the wilderness around them, without realizing that ownership loses meaning in the Canadian landscape.

Once Atwood said to me that Robert Frost's line "The land was ours before we were the land's" has no meaning in Canada.

In the thirteenth century, the great mystic Rumi wrote that "to praise is to praise the act of surrendering to the emptiness."

Sunday

We walk in the garden before breakfast, discussing a wall that needs to be repaired and what to plant by the side of the church. Since the beginning, we have felt not that we own this house but, rather, that we have been given it in trust, to look after, as if it were inconceivable to own something centuries old, and fruit trees that have grown out of the bones of ancient dead. On the last pages of *Surfacing*, the narrator says that her father must have realized in the end that he was an intruder in the wilderness: "the cabin, the fences, the fires and paths were violations; now his own fence excludes him, as logic excludes love."

On the radio this morning: Bush's army is at the gates of Baghdad. The soldiers force their way into the city under the banner of "liberators," freeing Iraq of a vicious dictator in order to install American control in the region. Under such circumstances, there is no moral distinction between figures such as Saddam and Bush; both are Agamemnon, pushing on for his own sake, confident that he is the chosen instrument of the gods, who will in turn privately reward him. Agamemnon is the father willing to sacrifice his own daughter, Iphigenia, for the sake of fair winds that will allow his fleet to reach Troy. According to Ovid, "the king sacrificed his paternal love for the sake of public interest." Scant consolation for Iphigenia.

In 1905, in a poem addressed to Roosevelt, the Nicaraguan poet Rubén Darío accused the United States of believing that "there where you put the bullet / You put the future.

"No," Darío bluntly concluded.

On television, a French journalist interviews a young English soldier shortly after his first killing: "Was this your first time in armed combat?" "Yes." "Were you frightened?" "You don't have time to be frightened. You do what you've been trained to do. You don't think about it." Except that now nothing can be the same for him ever again, for as long as he lives.

According to Kant, Reason and Madness are two neighboring realms whose borders are so close that it is impossible to explore one without straying into the other.

So it is in *Surfacing*. Halfway through the book, the narrator realizes that her explanation for her father's disappearance must be mistaken; that he did not become so obsessed with his research into rock paintings that he lost his mind in the wilderness. On the contrary. "I had the proof now, indisputable, of sanity and therefore of death. Relief, grief, I must have felt one or the other. A blank, a disappointment: crazy people can come back, from wherever they go to take refuge, but dead people can't, they are prohibited."

The Abnaki people of North America believe that a special group of deities, the Oonagamessok, presided over the making of rock paintings. The Abnaki explain the gradual disappearance of these paintings by saying that the gods are angry because of the lack of attention accorded to them since the arrival of the whites. The narrator's father (Atwood tells us) is a man riddled by stolid reason, and is less interested in the meaning of the rock paintings than in the materials with which they were created; he is someone who explains to his children that God is a superstition, "and a superstition—a thing that didn't exist. If you tell your children God doesn't exist they will be forced to believe you are the god, but what happens when they find out you are human after all, you have to grow old and die? Resurrection is like plants, Jesus Christ is risen today they sang at Sunday School, celebrating the daffodils; but people are not onions, as he so reasonably pointed out, they stay under."

Some Jews put little heaps of pebbles on the tombs of their dead in memory of the burials in the desert after the exodus from Egypt, when stones were used to mark the graves in the shifting sands. "It also prevents the dead from climbing out of their tombs again," a rabbi once told me, jokingly. The last time I visited my father's grave, I placed a heap of pebbles on the slab merely to mark my own passing. I now keep a couple of those pebbles in a wooden box in my library.

Monday

In Spanish, *Surfacing* translates as *Saliendo a la superficie*, or *Emergiendo* ("coming up to the surface" and "emerging"), both of which are clumsy and carry no music. Looking for a title for the Spanish translation, I suddenly think of *Alborada*, the surfacing of a new day.

What exactly is it that surfaces in *Surfacing*?

Tuesday

C. points to a swallow flying over the garden and skimming the pool. "It is an owl that has been trained by the Graces. It is a bat that loves morning light. It is the aerial reflection of a dolphin. It is the tender domestication of a trout." I wonder how many readers would guess that these lines are by John Ruskin.

In the post today, a letter from Peter Oliva in Calgary. I think of the endless Canadian landscapes and realize that the difference between those and what lies around me now, here in France, is essentially one of dimension. Here I feel as if I could simply stretch out my arm and touch a church, a copse, a hilltop. In Canada (as in Argentina) the horizon is always receding, what Drieu La Rochelle called horizontal vertigo.

Atwood: "We moved through flattened cow-sprinkled hills and leaf trees and dead elm skeletons, then into the needle trees and the cuttings dynamited in pink and grey granite and the flimsy tourist cabins, and the signs saying GATEWAY TO THE NORTH, at least four towns claim to be that. The future is in the North, that was a political slogan once; when my father heard it he said there was nothing in the north but the past and not much of that either."

In the European imagination, the Canadian north is blank; it is into this blankness that Frankenstein's Monster disappears at the end of Mary Shelley's novel.

Later

A large bee or a small bird flies in and out of the flowers C. has planted in the pots at the entrance. I think it's a tiny hummingbird, but I can't tell, it moves too fast. I need to know what it is before I can properly see it.

On one of the last pages of *Surfacing*:

> From the lake a fish jumps
> An idea of a fish jumps.

Earlier, as the narrator enters the northern Quebec of her childhood ("home ground, foreign territory"), she is filled with a sense of unreality: nothing seems the same as it once was. Perhaps that is our only true experience of our past: that whenever we revisit it, it (or our memory) has changed. We have as many autobiographies as moments of recollection.

In the introduction to her Cambridge lectures of last year, Atwood wrote, "We are all stuck in time, less like flies in amber—nothing so hard and clear—but like mice in molasses."

Wednesday

No one gets lost in the European landscape, except in fairy tales. Maybe they did in the Middle Ages, maybe they still do in a few secret corners of the Pyrenees or the Carpathians. But in the Europe I know there is always a road, a house in sight. I remember sitting by Lake Geneva and thinking how artificial its beauty is compared with the lakes I know in Canada. In Canada, Atwood's narrator says, "The lake is tricky, the weather shifts, the wind swells up quickly; people drown every year, boats loaded top-heavy or drunken fishermen running at high speed into dead-heads, old pieces of tree waterlogged and partly decayed, floating under the surface . . . Because of the convolutions it's easy to lose the way if you haven't memorized the landmarks." And also: "The small waves talking against the shore, multilingual water."

A poem by Gwendolyn MacEwen ends:

Explorer, you tell yourself this is not what you came for
Although it is good here, and green;
You had meant to move with a kind of largeness,
You had planned a heavy grace, an anguished dream.
But the dark pines of your mind dip deeper

And you are sinking, sinking, sleeper
In an elementary world;
There is something down there and you want to be told.

Thursday

Gray weather. I think of staying in the kitchen after breakfast, reading, but remember that today is the deadline for the review I have to write. I can't free myself from the conviction that I can relax only after having done my homework. The idea of spending the morning doing nothing but idling with a book that I don't *have* to read feels slightly obscene. I felt the same way as a child, telling myself I would play with my toy farm only after tidying my room, for instance.

I think Atwood's narrator shares this need. Early in her quest, she realizes that whatever end she is to attain, she must attain it through suffering: "We're here too soon and I feel deprived of something, as though I can't really get here unless I've suffered; as though the first view of the lake, which we can see now, blue and cool as redemption, should be through tears and a haze of vomit."

Saint Teresa, on the scorched soul seeking God's rain: "Do not weaken, unless you wouldst lose everything, for tears will win you all; one water brings on another."

Friday

First lunch in the garden this year.

Time magazine notes that an Iraqi Reconstruction Conference will take place in which private companies will bid for contracts of $25 billion to $100 billion to "rebuild" the Iraq the Anglo-Americans have bombed. According to *Time*, the planning of this conference began months before the first attack. Jean-Jacques Rousseau: "Hand over cash and soon you'll have them in irons."

Over the Canadian landscape of *Surfacing* the American presence looms invasively. Oddly, the resentment of the narrator's companions against Americans borders on caricature. "David says 'Bloody fascist pig Yanks,' as though he's commenting on the weather."

More than anything else, dialogue dates a novel.

While quick to make fun of Americans, like the narrator's companions, most Canadians are excruciatingly cautious in their criticism of others. Mostly, they seem possessed by what Carlyle called "the Pharisaical Brummellean Politeness, which would suffer crucifixion rather than ask twice for soup."

Sunday

Reports on the dead and wounded in Iraq keep pouring in. Images on television show a state of complete chaos. The Iraqi writer Jabbar Yussin Hussin describes the British tanks entering Basra and, by the side of the road, a terror-stricken young man, turning in all directions with his arms raised in the sign of surrender. The tanks rumble by and the young man puts his hands on his face, as if unable to believe he has survived, as if to make sure he is still alive. "Will he be allowed the freedom he can no longer bear? Or does he read in all this the uncertainty of his future?"

The narrator in *Surfacing* to the ghosts around her: "What sacrifice, what do they want?" That is always the question.

A ghost according to Joyce:

(Stephen's mother, emaciated, rises stark through the floor in leper grey with a wreath of faded orange blossoms and a torn bridal veil, her face worn and noseless, green with grave mould. Her hair is scant and lank. She fixes her bluecircled hollow eyesockets on Stephen and opens her toothless mouth uttering a silent word . . .) . . .
THE MOTHER: (*With the subtle smile of death's madness*) "I was once the beautiful May Goulding. I am dead."

Monday

Suddenly cool but still sunny. The cat has not come to be fed for almost three days now.

The narrator: "I cleared the table and scraped the canned ham fat scraps from the plates into the fire, food for the dead. If you fed them enough they would come back; or was it the reverse, if you fed them enough they would stay away, it was in one of the books but I'd forgotten."

My grandmother always used to kiss the bits of bread left over after a meal before throwing them away, as if the food we hadn't eaten belonged no longer to us but to others, to the dead perhaps, and she was required to show her respect for it. I think she felt some kind of continuity with all those who had gone before her and all those yet to come, and kissing the bread was an acknowledgment of their ghostly presence, of something or someone rooted in memory or in premonition. Perhaps she thought of this at the Passover meal, when she poured out a glass of wine for the prophet Elijah and then, according to tradition, opened the door saying the ritual words "Let all those who are hungry enter and eat."

Thursday

I show my library to the Argentine writer Alicia Borinsky. We stop at points of common recognition: early editions of Argentinian writers we both read in our adolescence—Silvina Ocampo, Cortázar, Oliverio Girondo. Then I point to Canadian writers she says she doesn't know: Sandra Birdsell, Sharon Butala, Anne Michaels, Andreas Schroeder, Susan Swan. A confession of secret pleasures in alphabetical order.

Which of Atwood's books will be considered classics in the future? *Surfacing*, *Alias Grace*, *The Handmaid's Tale*? A year before drowning herself in the River Ouse, Virginia Woolf asked in her diary, "Which of our friends will interest posterity most?" I would ask, instead, which among my secret writers will interest generations of readers to come? Richard Outram? Liliana Heker? Izaak Mansk? Rachel Ingalls? Phil Cousineau? James Hanley? John Hawkes?

Friday

The cat returned during the night.

Ways of ending.

Regarding the endings of stories, Walter Benjamin noted that, in keeping with Russian folk belief, the novelist Leskov "interpreted the Resurrection less as a transfiguration than as a disenchantment, in a sense akin to the fairy tales." The last pages of *Surfacing* are written, the reader feels, in exactly that fairy-tale tone. From the illusory world of men the narrator enters the true world of nature, of ghosts and ghostly presences. No redemption, no conclusion in the conventional sense, no "resurrection" but, rather, the termination of a bewitchment.

Atwood achieves this ending with astonishing simplicity. Bach explained that playing the clavier was very simple: you just had to strike the right key with the right strength at the right time.

Saturday

Throughout most of *Surfacing*, the real world appears to the narrator as haunted, incomprehensible; in the last chapter, the haunted world establishes itself as real, makes sense on its own terms. Escaping from the man-made world, the narrator runs naked through the woods like Frankenstein's Monster, a hunted animal, even believing that she will grow fur like a wild beast. "That is the way they are," she says of those who are now looking for her, "they will not let you have peace, they don't want you to have anything they don't have themselves."

The only contact she now wants is with the wilderness; she will not tread on the artificial path, "anything that metal has touched, scarred." Reversing the rituals of Robinson Crusoe (who founded his one-man society with the tools and books rescued from his shipwreck), the narrator enacts the ritual of a contrary foundation: she burns photographs and the Bible, smashes glasses and plates, rips scrapbooks, slashes linen and clothes. "Everything from history must be eliminated," she says.

Limping, bleeding, "resenting the gods although perhaps they saved me," she descends toward the lake, "skirting the worn places where shoes have been," and sees the ghost of her father. Or, rather, she sees that which her father has become, "the thing you meet when you've stayed here too long alone," but he shows no interest in her. Because she, too, has now embraced the wilderness, she has become not a wild creature but something stony or wooden, Daphne escaping from Apollo. A loon accepts her as a feature of the land. "I am part of the landscape, I could be anything, a tree, a deer skeleton, a rock." If the sacrifice a god makes is to take on human form, the sacrifice of a human is to become stone, twig, mud. The human Christ cleaves to Adam's tree.

Surfacing as Passion narrative.

Saint John of the Cross, describing Christ enamoured of the soul (as translated by Roy Campbell):

> Then, after a long time, a tree he scaled,
> Opened his strong arms bravely wide apart,
> And clung upon that tree till death prevailed,
> So sorely was he wounded in his heart.

MAY

Tuesday

It felt warm early this morning; I couldn't sleep so I got up and went into the library almost before dawn, waking the cat, who was not pleased.

My German publisher, Hans-Jürgen Balmes, suggests I compile an anthology on the theme of insomnia. I come up with a few bits and pieces:

- "He never attempted to sleep on his side, even in those dismal hours of the night when the insomniac longs for a third side after trying the two he has." Nabokov, *Pnin*.
- On a certain night, while he lay between sleep and wake, he would be overtaken by a long shuddering sigh, which he learned to know was the sign that his brain had once more conceived its horror, and in time—in due time—would bring it forth." Kipling, "In the Same Boat."
- "What is our insomnia if not the maniacal obstinacy of our intelligence to manufacture thoughts, chains of reasoning, syllogisms and definitions of its own, its refusal to abdicate in favour of the divine foolishness of eyes

shut fast or the wise madness of dreams? The man who does not sleep (and for the past few months I have been able to observe this on far too many occasions) more or less consciously refuses to trust the mere flow of things." Marguerite Yourcenar, *Memoirs of Hadrian*.

- "He was the solitary and lucid witness of a many-shaped world, instantaneous and almost intolerably precise . . . It was difficult for him to sleep. To sleep is to become distracted from the world." Borges, "Funes the Memorious."
- The title of a medieval Egyptian reference book: *Dawn for the Night-Blind*.
- "Sleepless night. The third in a row . . . I believe this sleeplessness comes only because I write. For however little or badly I write, I am still made sensitive by these minor shocks, I feel, especially towards the evening and even more in the morning, the nearby, imminent possibility of great moments which would rip me open, make me capable of anything, and in the turmoil within me and which I have no time to control I find no rest." Kafka, October 2, 1911.
- "Of restless sleep, streaked with continuous dreams, with frights and anxieties, was the night that preceded publication. Dawn broke at last and Luís Tinoco, though he was not an early riser, got up with the sun and went out to read his printed sonnet." Machado de Assis, "Dawn Without Day."

Not writing but reading keeps me awake. Reading is the occupation of the insomniac par excellence.

In the library it is cool. I look up at the books, just as the light starts to come in, and I have the comforting impression that they contain everything I want to know, as if they were an extension of my skin, tattooed like Queequeg's in *Moby-Dick* with "a complete theory of the heavens and the earth, and a mystical treatise on the art of attaining truth."

"Each season of life is an edition that amends the previous one, and that will in turn be amended, until the definitive edition is reached, of which the editor will present to the worms." For Machado de Assis we are, much like the insomniac books we read, full of paragraphs that need revising.

Wednesday

As well as their own secret signs, many of my books carry my signature, the date and place where I first read them, the marginal scribbles of my reading. I share this reflex of possession with the practitioners of other crafts: with architects who, since Garnier proudly inscribed his name on the cupola of the Paris Opera, sign their buildings; with salt-gatherers in the Camargue who autograph the lids of the boxes of the *fleur de sel* they have collected; with cabinetmakers who, just before finishing a piece, insert in a crack of the wood a slip of paper with their name and the date of completion.

Charlotte tells us the story of the local carpenter who built the shelves. The aptly named M. Dubois lacks all four fingers of his right hand. He was sawing a plank of wood and it slipped sideways toward the blade. A neighbor found him lying bleeding and unconscious on the workshop floor and took him to the hospital, but forgot to take the severed fingers. When M. Dubois returned, he found only one of the fingers. He picked it up and kept it on a shelf in his house, and he would point it out to visitors with ghoulish delight. One day he noticed that it, too, had disappeared; he assumed it had been carried away by a hungry mouse. Dutifully, M. Dubois wrote out the story of what had happened and inserted the slip of paper in the piece of furniture he had been making at the time of the accident.

For Machado de Assis (as for Diderot and for Borges), the title page of a book should carry the names of both the author and the reader, since they share its paternity.

"The worst defect of this book is you, reader," says Machado de Assis accusingly, halfway through *The Posthumous Memoirs of Brás Cubas* (which I pulled off the shelf on another sleepless night). "You are in a hurry to grow old and the book progresses all too slowly; you like your stories straightforward and packed with action, told in a measured and easy-flowing style, and this book and my style are like two drunkards, swaying from left to right, starting and stopping, complaining, shouting, laughing out loud, threatening heaven above, slipping and falling . . ."

Thursday

The Posthumous Memoirs of Brás Cubas is a hodgepodge of very brief chapters that are barely more than notes, snatches of dialogue, truncated love scenes, short character sketches and mini-essays, the lot building up the autobiography of a reluctant hero, the despondent Brás Cubas, already dead when the book begins.

Machado de Assis was a curious man. Born in 1839, he was the son of a Carioca mulatto painter and gilder, and of a white Portuguese washerwoman who worked for the widow of a senator and who died while Machado was still a small child. The aristocratic widow was chosen as the boy's godmother and the boy spent his childhood shifting between the poor and the rich household. His father remarried and it was his stepmother who taught him to read and write. Later, the neighborhood baker, who was from Paris, persuaded the boy to study French and to read the works of Lamartine and Victor Hugo. These two remained, throughout Machado's life, among his favorite authors. He grew up with a romantic, laconic, critical, ironic view of the world, evident on every page he wrote. "I grew up; my family had no hand in this. I grew naturally, as magnolia trees and cats grow."

In Brazil, Machado de Assis is classed among the Romantics, and yet I feel that his sensibility is deeply baroque. In baroque literature, something is true only if it means something else.

I have such great fondness for *The Posthumous Memoirs of Brás Cubas* that I'm always surprised to discover how few of my friends have read it. We assume that what delights us must delight others; in fact, we all realize in the end that our private circle of fellow readers, those who share our intimate loves, is very small. (Eleven friends attend the funeral of Brás Cubas as he begins to tell the story of his sorry life—only eleven.)

I count on my shelves five editions of *Brás Cubas* (three in translation) and several biographical studies. Considering the popularity of Sterne, of Pynchon (undeserved, I believe—I have no patience with him), of Cortázar, I find it hard to understand why Machado de

Assis remains (outside Brazil, of course) a secret writer. There is no one quite like him; all three authors I mentioned share with him a concern with how fiction should handle a fractured, time-riddled reality, but Machado de Assis is alone in telling a story that is allowed to show itself to the reader unassembled, as it were, like a Meccano kit, so that in the end it is up to us to put the parts together, constructing, as we read, a narrative that, though entirely comprehensible, follows no visibly pre-established pattern.

Machado's writing constantly subverts the reader's trust in the faithfulness of fiction. Reading him, I have the impression of watching a seemingly impossible conjuring trick. I see it, and yet I know it isn't real.

Chateaubriand would have approved of the very first sentence of *Brás Cubas*: "For some time I hesitated as to whether I should open these memoirs at the beginning or at the end; that is to say, whether I should place first my birth or my death." Machado chooses to begin at the last page. Is this the impulse that makes me flip to the back of a book to glimpse, however briefly, the last words first?

Monday

The Posthumous Memoirs of Brás Cubas is a perfect book to read when it is raining.

Unlike the heroes of Greek tragedies, whose fates are linked to those of past and future generations, Brás Cubas's sad story ends with his telling it. The last line of the book: "I did not bestow on any other creature the legacy of our misfortune."

Perhaps most novels could be called posthumous memoirs, since they are told only once the end has been reached. "Die! We all must die; all it takes is being alive." For Brás Cubas there is no sleep in death, only a kind of literary insomnia. Death is for him a point of departure, the moment in which we can conclusively consider life because there will be no more of it. He is, among other things, an incarnate memento mori. Not only is the protagonist dead from pneumonia at the beginning of the book; most of the other characters die as well. His mother suffers a slow and painful death; his first mistress, the Spanish Marcella, dies in the hospital of smallpox, lame Eugenia ends miserably; Eulalia succumbs to yellow fever on the day before their wedding; the husband of Virgilia, his second mistress, falls dead at the very moment of becoming a minister; Brás Cubas's best friend dies after realizing that his madness is incurable. Death, though rarely easy, allows Brás Cubas to intuit an answer to the ancient question of why we are born. As in a detective novel, the resolution of the mystery requires that someone be no more.

"I'll die," Machado de Assis once said, "as I've lived, with a book in my hand." According to José Veríssimo, who saw him in his final hours, Machado's last words were "Life is good." In *Brás Cubas* he wrote, "Frankness is a dead man's primary virtue."

Brás Cubas is dedicated "To the First Worm Who Gnawed on the Cold Flesh of My Corpse."

Tuesday

The cat pretends to be surprised by her tail, watches it for a while and then pounces to catch it. It is as if she has convinced herself of the apparition of something that looks like her tail but is not her tail: a fictional tail, so to speak. To enjoy the game, she allows herself the reader's willing suspension of disbelief.

Brás Cubas explains to the reader that his memoirs proceed from ideas that hang from the trapeze of his brain and demand his attention with the words "Decipher me or I'll devour you."

Devour: Bioy Casares recalled that the Argentinian writer Enrique Larreta once assured him "that his intelligence was so active that it did not allow him to read; each sentence would suggest to him a mass of ideas and images that led him astray through the worlds of his own mind and caused him to lose the thread of his reading."

Decipher: Today, during an interview on French radio, Catherine Henri, a teacher who has written a memoir of her high school experience, defined a good student as "one who allows himself to be astonished."

Sunday

I'm on the road again. I've traveled to the town of Umea, in northern Sweden, to give a lecture at the university. The hotel I'm staying at was a hospital in the 1800s, and ghastly photos of operating rooms, showing butcherlike doctors gathered around corpse-like patients, decorate the walls. I hear no comments on the war in Iraq here, as if the echoes of the conflict had died out in the distance. The landscape all around is Canadian: Regina or Winnipeg minus the skyscrapers. Waiting to be picked up, I sit in my room with *Brás Cubas*. The incongruity of reading a nineteenth-century Brazilian author at a distance of a hundred and fifty years, in an aseptic room in the far Scandinavian north on this Lutheran Sunday, does not escape me.

I imagine a volume of memoirs in the style of one of those bookbags that travelers used to carry with them centuries ago. An account of my life through the books I have read in the places I have visited. A task for my afterlife.

For Machado de Assis (or for Brás Cubas) the afterlife is the perfect place for self-reflection, because there we shall be all alone, with no witness. Unlike the crowded heavens and hells of Dante or Milton, Machado's are like the intellectual space created by a reader and a book: utterly private. For Brás Cubas, life is riddled with shame and "the foul vice" of hypocrisy, miseries caused by the presence of others. "But in death, what a difference! what a relief! . . . Because, essentially, in death there are no neighbours, no friends, no enemies, no acquaintances, no strangers: no public." Brás Cubas must tell his story from beyond the grave in order to leave a trace of his passing, which he feels was, like that of every other man, conducted in a crowded space under the indifferent glance of fellow travelers.

Nine years before he died in Paris, unknown and unread, the great Peruvian poet César Vallejo wrote in his notebook, "If, at the hour of a man's dying, all other men's pity were gathered to prevent him from doing so, that man would not die."

Monday

Stockholm. Impossible to get the shower to work. The main inconvenience of traveling is having to learn how to manipulate new bathroom fixtures.

The Posthumous Memoirs of Brás Cubas is a book of digressions, very much (as Machado acknowledges) in the vein of Laurence Sterne or Joseph de Maistre: "I believe the reader prefers story to reflection, like other readers, his colleagues, and I think he is right in doing so. We will get there. But I should say once more that this book is written with indolence, with the indolence of a man no longer concerned with the brevity of this century; it is a supinely philosophical work, of uneven philosophy, at times austere, at times playful, something that neither edifies nor destroys, neither freezes nor sets on fire, and is more than a pastime and less than an apostolate."

"Digressions, incontestably, are the sunshine; — they are the life, the soul of reading; — take them out of this book for instance, — you might as well take the book along with them." Sterne, in *Tristram Shandy*.

When Sterne died, only his bookseller was in attendance at the funeral. Weeks later, students in an anatomy course at Cambridge University were horrified to discover that the unearthed cadaver they were dissecting was that of the celebrated author of *Tristram Shandy*. Sterne's remains were sent back to the graveyard for reburial.

But digression does not mean jotting down everything. *Brás Cubas* is built up from carefully chosen digressions that allow room for the reader in the blanks between the nutshell chapters (for instance, between the memorable chapter made up of a list of words that cumulatively describe the funeral of Brás's father, and the chapter that transcribes a dialogue between Brás and Virgilia, made up entirely of punctuation marks).

In Samuel Butler's *Note-books*: "If a writer will go on the principle of stopping everywhere and anywhere to put down his notes, as the true painter will stop anywhere and everywhere to sketch, he will be able to cut down his works liberally. He will become prodigal not of writing—any fool can be this—but of omission. You become brief because you have more things to say than time to say them in. One of the chief arts is that of knowing what to neglect."

At dinner, the editor Anders Björnsson tells me that when a fire destroyed his entire library he suddenly felt that, in order to assemble one again, he first needed to know what books *not* to include.

Tuesday

Back home. Rain again. There is a reassuring feeling in this unchanging weather, as if its constancy in time underlined the constancy of place, making me feel welcome.

How odd that in so little time (barely two years) the house has acquired a personal past that concerns me, a history of our intimacy. Now every moment here is not only the experience of whatever is taking place but also the memories that cling to it. It is as if, more or less consciously, we laid away present moments to draw upon them later, like funds in an old-age pension. "Ungrateful reader," says Machado, "if you don't keep the letters you have written in your youth, you will not know one day the philosophy of old pages, you will not enjoy the pleasure of seeing yourself far away, in the shadows, with a three-cornered hat, seven-league boots and a long Assyrian beard, dancing to the rhythm of anacreontic bagpipes."

And earlier: "Believe me, the lesser evil is to remember; no one should trust present happiness; there is in it a drop of Cain's spittle. Once time has passed and the spasm ceased, then yes, then perhaps we can truly enjoy ourselves, because between one and the other of these two illusions, the better one is that which gives pleasure without pain."

Our neighbor comes to offer us some of his wood. He has calculated how much he will need if he lives to be ninety; all the rest he will give away.

Wednesday

My reading attaches itself to everything I do, to every place I visit. Brás Cubas travels to Portugal to study in Coimbra. When, a few years ago, I first saw that ancient city, with its magnificent cathedrals and exquisite baroque library, I felt less the weighty presence of history (wandering through Portugal's oldest university; visiting the House of Tears, where Inés de Castro, the beautiful wife of the infante Pedro, was murdered in 1355) than the fleeting ghost of the young Brás Cubas, who, for scarcely a paragraph, attended its august seat of learning. It seems to me that as I read I am taking notes, without knowing it, for what I will one day experience, or what I once experienced but failed to understand.

A French publisher has brought out a volume of pieces by a nineteenth-century Czech writer, Ladislav Klima, of whom I knew nothing. He seems to me like a Machado de Assis character: student of Schopenhauer and Nietzsche, inventor of a dubious tobacco substitute, steam-engine conductor, journalist, night watchman at a condemned factory, amateur philosopher. He left behind an immense hoard of manuscripts in Czech, German and Latin. Concerning the urge to understand our experience of the world, Klima argues, "Instead of saying, 'I seek the meaning of the world,' i.e., the superlative of all superlatives (and the very minute I pronounce the word, I have it, I achieve my purpose merely by having pronounced it), human philosophy has acted like the fool who would run through the streets in tears, looking for his own head on every street corner."

My reading colors my experience not only in the world but also on the page. I am often startled at finding the voice of one author I've read in another quite different author, the two removed from each other by continents and ages. This is Machado de Assis speaking up in Muriel Spark's very British first novel, *The Comforters*:

> It is possible for a man matured in religion by half a century of punctilious observance, having advanced himself in devotion the slow and exquisite way, trustfully ascending

his winding stair, and, to make assurance doubly sure, supplementing his mediations by deep-breathing exercises twice daily, to go into a flat spin when faced with some trouble which does not come within a familiar category.

Friday

On a day-trip to Turin for a get-together of Canadian writers, a charming Italian woman greets me by saying, "Welcome to Turin, Mr. Martel." I decide I'm too tired to contradict her and spend the day under Yann Martel's name, all sorts of people saying to me how much they like *Life of Pi*. That evening, when Yann arrives, I tell him not to be surprised if people remark on how much younger he looks now than he did in the morning.

In the newspaper, I read that a group of hackers have broken into the Romanian finance ministry's Web site and introduced a "tax on stupidity," to be levied in direct proportion to the importance of the position held. The site remains down while efforts are made to restore it to its former condition.

For Machado de Assis, stupidity is the essence of the human condition: "It is an old trick of Stupidity to become enamoured with other people's houses, so that, when she takes one over, it is very difficult to throw her out. And what a trick! She can't be dislodged, she lost all shame a long time ago. And if we consider the great number of houses she now occupies, many continuously, others only during the summer holidays, we must reach the conclusion that this amiable wanderer is truly the scourge of all landlords."

Sunday

Like Voltaire, Machado ironically proposes a philosophy of optimism, through the character of the destitute thinker Quincas Borba—a philosophy Borba calls Humanitism, which argues that pain is illusory. Chesterton: "The person who is really in revolt is the optimist, who generally lives and dies in a desperate and suicidal effort to persuade all the other people how good they are . . . Every one of the great revolutionists, from Isaiah to Shelley, have been optimists. They have been indignant, not about the badness of existence, but about the slowness of men in realizing its goodness."

Monday

A short night full of dreams. I give up trying to fall asleep again.

I often have dreams that take place in the library. Last night I dreamt that, as I walked in, the room was full of people, mostly writers whom I had known and who are now dead. I was overjoyed to see Denise Levertov and went over to kiss her, but she turned away with a smile and then started pulling books off my shelves and tossing them merrily in the air. I was afraid she'd hit someone.

In one of his journals, Gide tells of a dream in which he visits Proust in his library. Suddenly, his attention is drawn to a piece of string attached to some of the books. He pulls and several volumes fall, badly damaging their spines. "It's nothing," Proust says, with exquisite kindness and the attitude of a gentleman. "It's an edition of Saint-Simon of . . . ," and gives a date. At once, Gide recognizes that the book he has damaged is one of the rarest and most sought-after editions ever published.

Tuesday

The warm days have started. The wisteria over the entrance is in full bloom. Following Mavis's advice, C. has planted a large bed of cosmos flowers, a name that, according to the *Oxford English Dictionary*, was first used in 1650: "As the greater World is called Cosmus from the beauty thereof." The universe named after a flower.

I'm looking for a sundial to place on a pedestal that stands in the garden. When I find it, I'll inscribe a motto on it, such as "This Too Will Pass" or "All Wound, the Last One Kills." Or perhaps:

> I am a sundial. No words
> Can express my thoughts on birds.

Later

The wallpaper in my room at the Hôtel des Grands Hommes in Paris (where I stayed on my way back from Turin) had an eighteenth-century design with three separate mottoes. First, inscribed under a woman sitting among ruins, watching a solemn dog: "Friendship is not afraid of Time." Then, as Father Time is rowed across a stream by Cupid: "Love makes Time pass." Finally, while Cupid (asleep) is rowed across the same stream by Father Time: "Time makes Love pass."

To chronicle the passing of love and time, flowing back from the afterlife present, Machado de Assis merely places a bookful of random memoirs and observations in the hands of his readers. It is up to them to make his recollections theirs, to approve or disapprove of what he has done, to leave off at any chapter, to connect or not the scattered snapshots. Machado expects from his readers the constancy of friendship.

The obvious central theme of *The Posthumous Memoirs of Brás Cubas* is love: the nature of love, the persistence of love, the fading and transformation of love, the rediscovery of love after it has disappeared, past all expectation. Thinking of the women he has loved (the Spanish Marcella, his sister Sabina, his idealized Virgilia), Brás Cubas says he recalls them "as if these names and persons were only different aspects of my own affections"—much as Machado expects readers to recognize the phantoms of their own thoughts and passions on the page, like spectators in "the very serious matter of the theatre."

Up to a certain point, this is true of every book we love. We think we approach it from a distance, watch it part its protecting covers, observe the unfolding of its tale from a safe seat in the audience, and we forget how much the survival of the characters, the very life of the story, depends on our presence as readers—on our curiosity, on our desire to recall a detail or to be surprised by an absence—as if our own capacity for love had created, from a tangle of words, the person of the beloved.

I don't know yet to what book Machado's words will lead me.

READING LIST

June: *The Invention of Morel* by Adolfo Bioy Casares
July: *The Island of Dr. Moreau* by H. G. Wells
August: *Kim* by Rudyard Kipling
September: *Memoirs from Beyond the Grave* by François-René de Chateaubriand
October: *The Sign of Four* by Arthur Conan Doyle
November: *Elective Affinities* by Johann Wolfgang von Goethe
December: *The Wind in the Willows* by Kenneth Grahame
January: *Don Quixote* by Miguel de Cervantes
February: *The Tartar Steppe* by Dino Buzzati
March: *The Pillow Book* by Sei Shonagon
April: *Surfacing* by Margaret Atwood
May: *The Posthumous Memoirs of Brás Cubas* by Joaquim Maria Machado de Assis

ACKNOWLEDGMENTS

Thanks to early readers of the diary: Alice Manguel, Edith Sorel, Susan Swan, Katherine Ashenburg, Marie-Catherine Vacher, Hans-Jürgen Balmes, Michèlle Lapautre, Derek Johns, Carmen Criado, Jonathan Galassi, Gena Gorrell, and most especially Louise Dennys. And to the team at WCA, as always.